Presented To

_____

From

_____

Date

_____

365
MOMENTS
of PEACE *for a*
WOMAN'S
HEART

REFLECTIONS ON GOD'S GIFTS OF
LOVE, HOPE, AND COMFORT

BETHANYHOUSE

a division of Baker Publishing Group
Minneapolis, Minnesota

Copyright © 2005, 2006, 2007, 2008, 2009, 2010, 2011 by GRQ Inc.

Readings extracted from previously published volumes *Moments of Peace for the Morning, Moments of Peace for the Evening, Quiet Moments Alone With God, Moments of Peace from the Psalms, Moments of Peace for a Woman's Heart, Psalms to Soothe a Woman's Heart, Moments of Peace in the Presence of God for Couples, Moments of Peace in the Widom of God*

Published by Bethany House Publishers
11400 Hampshire Avenue South
Bloomington, Minnesota 55438
www.bethanyhouse.com

Bethany House Publishers is a division of
Baker Publishing Group, Grand Rapids, Michigan

Printed in China

ISBN 978-0-7642-1298-7

Scripture quotations identified AMP are from the Amplified® Bible, copyright © 1954, 1958, 1962, 1964, 1965, 1987 by The Lockman Foundation. Used by permission.

Scripture quotations identified CEV are from the Contemporary English Version © 1991, 1992, 1995 by American Bible Society. Used by permission.

Scripture quotations identified ESV are from The Holy Bible, English Standard Version® (ESV®), copyright © 2001 by Crossway, a publishing ministry of Good News Publishers. Used by permission. All rights reserved. ESV Text Edition: 2007

Scripture quotations identified GNT are from the Good News Translation—Second Edition. Copyright © 1992 by American Bible Society. Used by permission.

Scripture quotations identified GOD'S WORD are from GOD'S WORD®. © 1995 God's Word to the Nations. Used by permission of Baker Publishing Group.

Scripture quotations identified HCSB are from the Holman Christian Standard Bible, copyright 1999, 2000, 2002, 2003 by Holman Bible Publishers. Used by permission.

Scripture quotations identified ICB are from the International Children's Bible. Copyright © 1986, 1988, 1999 by Tommy Nelson™ a division of Thomas Nelson, Inc. Used by permission. All rights reserved.

Scripture quotations identified KJV are from the King James Version of the Bible.

Scripture quotations identified THE MESSAGE are from *The Message* by Eugene H. Peterson, copyright © 1993, 1994, 1995, 2000, 2001, 2002. Used by permission of NavPress Publishing Group. All rights reserved.

Scripture quotations identified NASB are from the New American Standard Bible®, copyright © 1960, 1962, 1963, 1968, 1971, 1972, 1973, 1975, 1977, 1995 by The Lockman Foundation. Used by permission.

Scripture quotations identified NCV are from the New Century Version®. Copyright © 1987, 1988, 1991 by Word Publishing, a division of Thomas Nelson, Inc. Used by permission. All rights reserved.

Scripture quotations identified NIrV are from the Holy Bible, New International Reader's Version®. NIrV®. Copyright © 1995, 1996, 1998 by Biblica, Inc.™ Used by permission of Zondervan. All rights reserved worldwide. www.zondervan.com

Scripture quotations identified NIV are taken from the HOLY BIBLE, NEW INTERNATIONAL VERSION®. Copyright © 1973, 1978, 1984 Biblica. Used by permission of Zondervan. All rights reserved.

Scripture quotations identified NKJV are from the New King James Version. Copyright © 1982 by Thomas Nelson, Inc. Used by permission. All rights reserved.

Scripture quotations identified NLT are from the *Holy Bible*, New Living Translation, copyright © 1996, 2004, 2007 by Tyndale House Foundation. Used by permission of Tyndale House Publishers, Inc., Carol Stream, Illinois 60188. All rights reserved.

Scripture quotations identified NLV are taken from the Holy Bible, New Life™ Version Copyright © 1969–2003 by Christian Literature International, PO Box 777, Canby, OR 97013. Used by permission.

Scripture quotations identified NRSV are from the New Revised Standard Version of the Bible, copyright © 1989, by the Division of Christian Education of the National Council of the Churches of Christ in the United States of America. Used by permission. All rights reserved.

Scripture quotations identified TLB are from *The Living Bible*, copyright © 1971. Used by permission of Tyndale House Publishers, Inc., Wheaton, Illinois 60189. All rights reserved.

Cover design by Eric Walljasper
Interior design by Kevin Ferguson

15   16   17   18   19   20   7   6   5   4

CONTENTS

Introduction   7

January   9
February   41
March   71
April   105
May   137
June   171
July   203
August   237
September   269
October   301
November   335
December   367

INTRODUCTION

Would you be surprised to learn that God loves you? He does! He loves you with all his heart, and he knows you better than you know yourself. That's because you are his creation, his handiwork, the expression of his artistic genius. He knows about your struggles and your achievements. He knows about your secret acts of kindness and your secret sins. He knows what you need and what you don't need. He knows, and he wants you to know too—both who you are and who he is.

365 Moments of Peace for a Woman's Heart was written for that purpose. It opens the door wide to knowing God and becoming the woman he created you to be. When you look into his face and see your reflection in his loving eyes, you'll receive strength to overcome fears and obstacles, discover new ways of thinking, and develop the skills to walk in new and exciting paths.

It is our prayer that as you read, you will see and understand God's wonderful plan for you, a plan designed to reveal your incredible worth and beauty. In seeking, you will find more treasure than you ever imagined.

JANUARY

*When you call upon me
and come and pray to me, I will
hear you. When you search for me,
you will find me; if you seek me
with all your heart.*

JEREMIAH 29:12–13 NRSV

GOD'S DELIGHT

For Yahweh takes pleasure in His people; He adorns the humble with salvation. Let the godly celebrate in triumphal glory; let them shout for joy.

Psalm 149:4–5 HCSB

There may be times in your life when you feel as if you're on your own—it seems that no one understands or cares for you, and you can't do anything right. These are the times it is most important to remember your Creator. God loves you, cares for you, and works through you to fulfill his purpose for your life.

Of course, he does not approve of your sins, because when you commit them you hurt yourself. That's why he empowers you to turn from them and triumph over them.

Are you feeling like a failure today? Rejected, unloved, and unworthy? Then it's time to give up your opinion of yourself and embrace God's vision for your life. He delights in you and will lead you to victory if you will follow him.

God, in you is all my worth, glory, and joy. I thank you for accepting and loving me. I praise you for delighting in me and leading me to victory. Amen.

Sing to the Lord a new song, and His praise in the congregation of the godly ones.

Psalm 149:1 NASB

RIGHT LIVING

Jesus came to them and said . . . "Go and make disciples of all nations . . . teaching them to obey everything I have commanded you."

Matthew 28:18–20 NIV

Though God's rules may never win a popularity contest, he has given them for pure and noble purposes to those who are willing to listen.

God, lover of peace and harmony, sets guidelines for you to follow in your relationships with your family, friends, co-workers, acquaintances, and fellow citizens of this world. He desires fairness and justice for all, and he shows you how to achieve those ends, even when doing so might prove inconvenient for you.

God, lover of the highest good, implores you to put his commandments into practice, because when you do, all his gifts, benefits, and blessings fill your life.

Happy are those who fear the Lord, who greatly delight in his commandments.

Psalm 112:1 NRSV

Dear God: Put in me a willing and obedient spirit, and grant me the wisdom to listen to your teachings and apply your commandments to my thoughts, words, and actions. Amen.

January 3

RESPITE FOR THE
WEARY SOUL

*He who dwells in the shelter of the Most High will rest in the
shadow of the Almighty.*

Psalm 91:1 NIV

How does one rest in the shadow of the Almighty? The idea presented is this: You are in the presence of God no matter where you are or what time of the day it happens to be. God is always with you, and his presence brings you an undeniable sense of peace.

This means that you can abide in his shelter at all times—sensing his closeness and deep affection no matter the situation. Whether you are shopping, in a business meeting, talking with a friend, or praying at home in your quiet time, he is with you.

When heartache threatens or trouble approaches, his protective cover drops down over your life, providing the spiritual comfort you need amid every storm.

God, thank you for protecting me from the troubles that assail me. I am tired, Lord, but I am thankful that with you I can find true rest. Amen.

He will cover you with his feathers. He will shelter you with his wings. His faithful promises are your armor and protection.

Psalm 91:4 NLT

A MANTLE OF LOVE

Let all those who take refuge and put their trust in You rejoice; let them ever sing and shout for joy, because You make a covering over them and defend them.

Psalm 5:11 AMP

It has been speculated that intelligent women prefer to be perceived as physically attractive and that good-looking women wish to be seen as clever. Yet what most women truly desire is to be accepted. Adored. Cherished. Loved.

That's exactly what you are when you take refuge in God. As you spend time with him, he envelops you in his majesty and grace, and his splendor shines through you. You become not only pretty, but beautiful; not just smart, but wise. Not only accepted, adored, cherished, and loved—but merciful, gentle, joyful, and loving.

Therefore, instead of worrying about whether you are smart or pretty, rejoice that you're clothed in God's mantle of love. Because that, friend, is what makes you truly exceptional.

God, thank you for covering me with the mantle of your love. Your presence makes me beautiful and wise, and I praise you with all my heart. Amen.

You bless the godly, O Lord; you surround them with your shield of love.

Psalm 5:12 NLT

LEAN ON HIM

Trust in the Lord with all your heart. Do not depend on your own understanding.

Proverbs 3:5 NIrV

While the "independent woman" stands as an icon to self-sufficiency and personal savvy, her liberty is limited unless she humbly confesses her reliance on God.

God has blessed you with certain skills, resources, and opportunities, and he is pleased when you use these things to their fullest potential. As you do, you will find he entrusts you with even more marvelous gifts, and these, too, he has given you for your good and the benefit of others.

With your efforts, you develop into a woman who knows her own mind and handles her responsibilities well, a truly independent woman. It happens when you place your reliance on God.

You, Lord, give true peace to those who depend on you, because they trust you.

Isaiah 26:3 NCV

Dear God: I depend on you for the genuine independence of heart and mind I need to trust in you and learn your wondrous ways. Amen.

HE HEARS

The Lord has heard the voice of my weeping. The Lord has heard my supplication; the Lord will receive my prayer.

Psalm 6:8–9 NKJV

At times you may confide in people, and although they appear to be paying attention, they may not really grasp what you're telling them. They do not comprehend the depth of your emotions or the helplessness of your situation. Even if they can empathize with you, they will be unable to offer you genuine, lasting relief.

Yet when you call out to God, he truly hears you—even the words you don't say. He understands the pain you feel and is committed to giving you the most effective help with whatever you're facing.

Have you taken your troubles to others, only to be let down? Then turn your concerns over to God. He's always glad to listen and has promised never to fail you. Trust him.

O Lord, rescue my soul; save me because of Your lovingkindness.

Psalm 6:4 NASB

God, thank you for hearing my prayers — even the wordless ones that come from my heart. Truly, you are my most wonderful confidant, and I praise you. Amen.

GOD'S GOOD TIME

Restore to me the joy of your salvation, and sustain in me a willing spirit.

Psalm 51:12 NRSV

We're accustomed to getting things done in a hurry, and we purchase gadgets and appliances promising speed and convenience. As we learn more about God, however, we realize he keeps a different pace, moving in his own time and according to his highest purposes.

When you willingly wait on God for the desires of your heart, you expand and deepen your worship of him to include godly patience and trust. In your willing submission to his pace, you prove you truly have confidence in his wisdom and his timetable. Your peace of mind leaves you free to truly enjoy the moment, knowing and believing time belongs to God.

The Lord is good to those who wait for him, to the soul that seeks him.

Lamentations 3:25 NRSV

Heavenly Father: When I come before you with the desires of my heart, grant me the will to wait on you in quiet expectation and with godly hope. Amen.

WHY?

We have not stopped praying for you and asking God to fill you with the knowledge of his will through all spiritual wisdom and understanding.

Colossians 1:9 NIV

*I*f you have been in a tragic situation, you know what it's like to ask God why. God hears and uses your "why" to strengthen you and bring you his peace.

When you cry out to him, you are naming the burden of your heart and presenting him with the fullness of your emotions. Your straightforward prayer shows you are facing your fears and opening yourself to spiritual growth, insight, and maturity. As you meditate on his Word and listen for his answer, you discern where God would have you go from here.

Peace, founded on full surrender to God's purpose, is his compassionate answer to your cry of why.

I trust in you, O Lord; I say, "You are my God." My times are in your hand.

Psalm 31:14–15 NRSV

Heavenly Father: When I don't understand and my strength fails, grant me readiness to rely solely on your will and find peace in surrendering to your wisdom. Amen.

TRUE HEALING

O God of my righteousness! You have given me relief when I was in distress.

Psalm 4:1 ESV

Whether it is pain or paralysis in your limbs or an illness that affects you internally, health problems can severely limit what you can accomplish. The same is true for emotional and spiritual difficulties. Fears and regrets can torment you to the point that you feel trapped in your situation.

In your own power, you can do nothing to set yourself free; yet God can overcome whatever you are facing. In fact, God will work through your affliction to make you genuinely complete and help you fulfill your purpose in life.

God, thank you for truly healing my distress and giving relief to my troubled soul. I trust you to turn this place of pain into a reason for praising you. Amen.

Therefore, trust him to heal you to the depths of your soul. He will turn your limitations into opportunities for surprising fruitfulness and teach you how to live in his comfort and abundance.

You have given me greater joy than those who have abundant harvests of grain and new wine.

Psalm 4:7 NLT

ATTENTION, PLEASE

Keep your guard up. . . . Keep a firm grip on the faith.
1 Peter 5:9 THE MESSAGE

Imagine you're supervising a child who asks if she can walk to a friend's house several blocks away. You give your permission, but first you remind her of the traffic and warn her to pay close attention as she crosses a busy intersection.

In the Bible, God identifies sin so you will be fully aware of its dangers and the consequences of wrongdoing. Then he promises you his strength as you hold on to his words and rely on his warnings, applying his guidance and direction as you go forward with your life. Remain vigilant, he says, because vigilance will keep you safe from harm.

Heavenly Father: Grant me an attentive heart and a vigilant spirit so I will hear and heed your warnings offered to me in love. Amen.

Be very careful, then, how you live—not as unwise but as wise.
Ephesians 5:15 NIV

January 11

DON'T LOSE YOUR FOCUS

Our eyes look to the Lord our God.

Psalm 123:2 ESV

Everything changes when you set your focus on God. You filter every situation through the knowledge you have of him. Is any problem too hard for him? No. Can he use every circumstance for your good and his glory? Yes.

Because nothing is impossible for God, every challenge you encounter is just another opportunity to see his mighty work in your life—building your confidence in him.

Unfortunately, sometimes you lose your focus. It's so easy to do—especially when unexpected trouble arises. It can even be something small—a flat tire, a bill that's difficult to pay, an irritating issue. Suddenly you're wondering, *God, where are you?*

God hasn't moved; your focus has—and you must turn your attention back to him. Because he's *still* bigger than your problems and will certainly help you.

God, help me to keep my eyes on you! I praise you that nothing is ever too difficult for you and that you use everything for my good and your glory. Amen.

I lift my eyes to You, the One enthroned in heaven. . . . Show us favor, Lord.

Psalm 123:1, 3 HCSB

THROUGH HIM YOU WON'T FAIL

O my Strength, I watch for you; you, O God, are my fortress, my loving God. God will go before me.

Psalm 59:9–10 NIV

You face many challenges every day—some are exciting, some routine, and others may be quite difficult. While there are times of instability that will assail your life, there is one truth that never changes: God is your eternal strength and your present help. Nothing you face takes him by surprise.

God has never been unfaithful to you, and he never will be. If he has asked you to wait for his answer to come, then it is because he has something far better for you than you can imagine.

Thoughts of doubt may tempt you to believe that he is not watching over your life; however, if he knows when a sparrow falls to the earth, then he certainly knows your every need.

You've been a safe place for me. . . . Strong God, I'm watching you do it, I can always count on you—God, my dependable love.

Psalm 59:16–17 THE MESSAGE

God, thank you for loving me and for walking with me each moment of every day. No matter what I face, I know that you will help me through the day. Amen.

RIGHT AND WRONG

Therefore I do my best always to have a clear conscience toward God and all people.

Acts 24:16 NRSV

Many women avoid drawing a clear distinction between right and wrong for fear of appearing intolerant. They often find, however, their consciences are then clouded by doubt.

The Bible offers God's clear perspective. First, he wants you to know the difference between right and wrong, so he sets out his commandments and his will for your relationships and your actions. Second, he wants you to possess a conscience free of misgivings. He graces you with cleansing forgiveness and renewing strength so you can distinguish right from wrong freely and without reservation. Third, he invites you deeper into the Bible to discover more about his unchanging truth, wisdom, and holiness.

Dear God: Bathe my conscience in the wisdom of your Word and strengthen my resolve to live your principles of truth and justice. Amen.

This command is love, which comes from a pure heart and a good conscience and a sincere faith.

1 Timothy 1:5 NIV

A SURE DEFENDER

With my voice I cry to the Lord, and He hears and answers me out of His holy hill.

Psalm 3:4 AMP

As King David considered his options, he realized that there could be no good resolution to the conflict. His son Absalom had rallied forces to take the throne of Israel away from him. It was an impossible situation—either David would lose his kingdom and life or he would lose his son. No matter the outcome, his heart and his nation would be broken. Psalm 3 is the prayer that flowed from the anguish within him.

Are you facing a situation that seems completely hopeless? Go to God. Even if you cannot see a constructive way out, he can, and he knows exactly what is best for everyone involved. Therefore, trust him. He is your Shield and Defender, and if you obey him, he will surely lead you to triumph.

You are my shield, and you give me victory and great honor.

Psalm 3:3 CEV

God, thank you for not only hearing me but also for understanding my situation better than I do. I will trust you to guide me to the best solution. Amen.

AT HOME

[Jesus said:] "Look at me. I stand at the door. I knock. If you hear me call and open the door, I'll come right in and sit down to supper with you."

Revelation 3:20 THE MESSAGE

hink of a place where you feel most at home. Perhaps it's a cozy corner of a favorite room, or a spot outside where you savor the view and the sounds of nature. Now you have a sense of God's feelings as he finds a place in your heart.

Dear God: Thank you for entering my life with your divine presence. Keep me ever mindful of you, my heart's most honored guest. Amen.

Like the most gracious of guests, God enters in peace and goodwill, and puts himself at your service. He listens as you speak, cares about what you're going through, and offers his support, encouragement, and partnership. As your faith opens your heart to him, he opens his strength and wisdom to you.

Your divine guest feels right at home in you.

[Jesus said,] "Indeed, the kingdom of God is within you."

Luke 17:21 NKJV

January 16

TIME IN HIS PRESENCE

Blessed (happy, fortunate, and to be envied) are all those who seek refuge and put their trust in Him!

Psalm 2:12 AMP

Knowing God is a privilege. Although some have the good fortune of meeting with presidents and prime ministers, few are invited into their inner sanctuary—and no one is eternally changed by the encounter.

Yet God invites you to know him in the most profound way possible and to embrace his best for your life. The Creator of the universe beckons you to be transformed by his divine mercy, wisdom, and provision, and to know the unlimited power and love that have been made available to you.

Spending time in God's presence is a precious gift—one that you have been given to enjoy at any moment, no matter the hour or the reason. Therefore, do not decline his invitation. It is the best appointment you will keep all day.

Worship God in adoring embrace, celebrate in trembling awe.

Psalm 2:11 THE MESSAGE

God, thank you so much for inviting me into your presence, transforming my life, and loving me. I praise and worship you with all of my heart. Amen.

A TEACHABLE MOMENT

We should make plans—counting on God to direct us.

Proverbs 16:9 TLB

*Y*ou know the feeling—you had everything planned, then something happened along the way to turn your plans inside out. You could think of these times as God's teachable moments.

> *Heavenly Father:*
> *In your love, grant*
> *me the willingness to*
> *adapt my plan to your*
> *plans, my time to your*
> *purposes, my desires to*
> *your will. Amen.*

While God commends you for formulating good and responsible plans, he also wants you to remain responsive to the changes and challenges of life. Some changes strengthen you, others broaden your perspective and expertise. Some of life's challenges surprise you, startle you, amaze you, or even mystify you. All, however, come to you as opportunities from God to walk ever more closely with him.

Let the next "teachable moment" find you open to God's good plans for you.

My times are in Your hand.

Psalm 31:15 NKJV

A BIBLICAL MIND

God wants the combination of his steady, constant calling and warm, personal counsel in Scripture to come to characterize us.

Romans 15:4 THE MESSAGE

God promises to keep you mindful of his words, but for him to remind you, you need to know what he has said. For this reason, your continued growth and maturity as a Christian comes with a practical and practicable Bible study plan.

How long you spend in God's Word depends on what you're able to accomplish. Five minutes of attentive reading achieves more than an hour of study planned but never spent. You can find Bible study aids in bookstores and online, along with commentaries to explain meaning and context. Also, group Bible study works to keep you committed and accountable, and also offers the gift of Christian fellowship.

> Jesus said to them . . . "Others, like seed sown on good soil, hear the word, accept it, and produce a crop—thirty, sixty or even a hundred times what was sown."
>
> Mark 4:13, 20 NIV

Dear God: Teach me to know and love you through your Word, and grant me the godly commitment I need to learn from you. Amen.

WAITING FOR JUSTICE

Judge me and show that I am honest and innocent. You know every heart and mind, and you always do right.

Psalm 7:8–9 CEV

*I*t can be truly disheartening when others advance because of the lies they have told about you. That is what happened to David. Those who were jealous of his success accused him of treason. With his life in danger and no way to defend himself, David turned to the only One he could truly count on: God. David was confident that the Lord would defend him and prove his innocence.

God, thank you for seeing my innocence and for defending me. However long it takes, I trust you to bring justice out of this situation. Amen.

Are you powerless to counteract the false charges of others? Are their allegations endangering your future? Do not fear. Just as God defended David, he will protect you as well. Therefore, continue to honor God in every aspect of your life, and be patient. His justice is coming, and soon everyone will know the truth.

You, God, are my shield, the protector of everyone whose heart is right.

Psalm 7:10 CEV

January 20

THE RIGHT THING

Wait on the Lord; be of good courage, and He shall strengthen your heart.

Psalm 27:14 NKJV

We owe our gratitude to the untold numbers of women who have stood up for justice and truth. Because their voices were heard, laws changed, attitudes shifted, and educational and workplace opportunities opened and expanded for the generations that followed them.

In your own life, you demonstrate that same great courage when you choose what you know is right despite the difficulty, unpopularity, or likely consequences of your choice. Your own strength may falter when hardships come, and you may wonder if it's worth the struggle. God says "Yes, it is," and he will supply the courage you need if you rely on him when the time comes.

[The Lord said:] "Be strong and very courageous."

Joshua 1:7 NASB

Dear God: Grant me the strength of heart and the courage to do the right thing. I need your help to stand firm against all opposition. Amen.

TO BE BLESSED

Happy are those who . . . love the Lord's teachings, and they think about those teachings day and night.

Psalm 1:1–2 NCV

When you have a wounded heart, you may find it difficult to know where to turn. You look outwardly to loved ones and those who purport to know the answers to your hurt, but there is no real comfort. You look into yourself and find pain and confusion there. Where can you go to soothe your soul?

God, I need you. Thank you for revealing yourself to me through the Psalms and for healing my heart. Only you can truly bless me. Amen.

Friend, it is no coincidence that your search has brought you to the Psalms. It is not in looking out or in, but *up* to God that you will find what you are seeking. God promises you blessings when you read and embrace the Bible; God promises that you will be filled with love, joy, purpose, and peace. Isn't that what your heart has been aching for, after all?

They are strong, like a tree planted by a river. The tree produces fruit in season, and its leaves don't die. Everything they do will succeed.

Psalm 1:3 NCV

IN TIMES OF PERIL

God guards you from every evil, he guards your very life. He guards you when you leave and when you return, he guards you now, he guards you always.

Psalm 121:7–8 THE MESSAGE

Are you facing a situation that terrifies you? Perhaps you've pondered the consequences of a misstep and the possible pain ahead, and it's more than you can handle. The anxiety churns within you—stealing your sleep and consuming your thoughts.

Take comfort in the words of Psalm 121:7 (THE MESSAGE), "God . . . guards your very life." You perceive no help from anywhere around you, but it's because you've failed to rely upon the One who can truly deliver you. You must look to God and trust him to defend you.

You have Someone who is fighting for you—who loves, provides for, and protects you in every circumstance of life. So have faith in him. Lift your eyes to God and realize that help is on the way.

> *God, you know how difficult and upsetting my situation is. Help me to trust you in and through this. Nothing is impossible for you, and so my heart will rest in your care. Amen.*

I lift up my eyes to the hills. From where does my help come? My help comes from the Lord, who made heaven and earth.

Psalm 121:1–2 ESV

MARK YOUR WORDS

Those who speak with care will be rewarded.
Proverbs 18:21 NCV

From early childhood, we begin to understand the power of words. We learn how words can please others, make friends, solve problems, and comfort hurting hearts. In the Bible, God calls to mind these truths.

The words you use reflect your attitude and feelings toward others, and well-chosen, timely words show your positive engagement with the world around you. When you express yourself for the purpose of building up people, contributing to the common well-being, and advancing worthy causes, your communication advances God's work in the world.

Even when you aren't talking about God, your godly words reflect your discipleship and prove an effective witness to his work in your life.

To make an apt answer is a joy to anyone, and a word in season, how good it is!
Proverbs 15:23 NRSV

Dear God: When I communicate with others, help me choose words with care and compassion so they reflect your gracious words of love to me. Amen.

YOUR NOT-SO-SECRET WEAPON

With God's help we will do mighty things.
Psalm 60:12 NLT

t first glance, a task may seem too great for you. You try to make a schedule, but confusion and fear set in. Before you know it, you feel tempted to run. However, deep within your heart, God is saying, "Stay where you are. Trust me. I'll help you."

God's desire is to guide you at every turn in life, and he has promised to lead you past places of difficulty and extreme pressure in order to prove his faithfulness. You never have to be afraid, because he promises to provide all you need.

Are you facing an overwhelming challenge today? Have faith in the One who has all you need to achieve the victory. He will not fail you; rather, he will lead you to triumph—so trust him.

God, there are times when I feel overwhelmed by the circumstances of life, but I know you have promised to do mighty things in and through me when I trust you. Amen.

Use your powerful arm and give us victory.
Then the people you love will be safe.

Psalm 60:5 CEV

January 25

GOD'S ANSWER

*Call to Me, and I will answer you, and show you great and mighty
things, which you do not know.*

Jeremiah 33:3 NKJV

Are you a woman who is open to new ideas—someone who longs to discover new things about God and his ways? That kind of willingness to learn pleases God, and he urges us to explore even further by speaking to him in prayer.

When you spend time in prayer, you take advantage of the extraordinary privilege of placing your concerns, hopes, anxieties, and plans in God's hands. True to his promise, he takes them up as quickly as you release them, and he assures you he cares and understands. Then he says to you, "I know how all this will turn out. Watch and listen, while I show you."

*Heavenly Father:
Thank you for the gift
of prayer and its power
to change the way I
think, act, and feel.
Amen.*

The Lord . . . delights in the prayers of his people.

Proverbs 15:8 TLB

34

January 26

WHY SHOULD HE CARE?

*When I look at the night sky and see the work of your fingers—
the moon and the stars you set in place—what are . . . human
beings that you should care for them?*

Psalm 8:3–4 NLT

*S*ometimes it is surprising to discover how deeply and
sincerely you are loved. Perhaps you even find others' devotion difficult to accept because you are accustomed to
thinking of yourself as unlovable or unworthy.

This may be especially true when considering God's perfect,
unconditional love. After all, he is majestic and holy—capable
of creating the world and everything in it. Surely there are better,
more worthy creatures to love, right?

Not to God.

If you have ever wondered *why* God loves you, then realize you
are pondering the wrong question. God's nature is love, and he created you for the glorious purpose of
expressing his wonderful, unlimited
care for you. Therefore, accept it! Because there is nothing you could ever
do to make him stop loving you.

*My God, thank you
so much for loving me
unconditionally! Help
me to accept the reality
of your love with all
my heart, soul, mind,
and strength. Amen.*

O Lord, our Lord, how majestic is Your
name in all the earth, who have displayed Your splendor above the heavens!

Psalm 8:1 NASB

FAR SIGHTED

"My thoughts are not your thoughts, neither are your ways my ways," declares the Lord.

Isaiah 55:8 NIV

Now that you're an adult, you see things differently than when you were a little girl. You possess a perspective unavailable to you before, a perspective that continues to broaden and deepen as you embrace more of life. Even if you live to a grand old age, however, you will never gain God's vast perspective.

O God: When I don't understand, keep me mindful of your infinite wisdom; and when I don't see, help me remember your eternal point of view. Amen.

Consider where God has been—before time began, when he created the world. Throughout history he was there. Meditate on what he sees—before you were born, he saw you and saw each day of your life. No wonder his ways seem mysterious! God's perspective includes earth and heaven and eternity.

Let God transform you into a new person by changing the way you think.

Romans 12:2 NLT

UNLIMITED POSSIBILITIES

It is required that those who have been given a trust must prove faithful.

1 Corinthians 4:2 NIV

God never asks for the impossible, but he often makes the impossible happen when someone uses the abilities and resources he has provided.

You possess everything you need to perform what God requires of you this day, and for that reason, how you use his gifts matters to him. He insists on accountability, because he knows that your mindful assessment of your gifts and how you will use them does two things. First, it compels your gratitude to God for all he has given to you; and second, it encourages you to identify and develop your gifts to the fullest.

See what's possible when you use what he has provided.

> Good stewards of the manifold grace of God, serve one another with whatever gift each of you has received.
>
> 1 Peter 4:10 NRSV

Dear God: Thank you for the abilities and resources you have seen fit to give me. Keep me committed to their continual development and constant use. Amen.

HONEY-DO

Let the loveliness of our Lord, our God, rest on us, confirming the work that we do. Oh, yes. Affirm the work that we do!

Psalm 90:17 THE MESSAGE

God may lift you up and give you a position of great responsibility. He may allow you to be like the men in David's army, who stayed at base camp while the others rode off to fight the enemy.

Obeying him is the most important thing you will ever do. Never compare your effort to that of another. Instead, ask him to confirm you.

Are you doing what the Lord has called you to do? Do you find joy in being in the middle of his will? Can you say with confidence, "Lord, I have done my best; bless the work of my hands"?

A great sense of peace is gained by simply being what he wants you to be regardless of what this does or does not entail.

Lord God, I lift my heart up to you in praise and worship. Thank you for giving me wonderful assignments to do for your name's sake. Amen.

Let us, your servants, see your mighty deeds; let our descendants see your glorious might.

Psalm 90:16 GNT

January 30

EXPECT THE BEST

My soul, wait silently for God alone, for my expectation is from Him.

Psalm 62:5 NKJV

Many women anticipate great things, while other women anticipate great things and set about to make them happen. Which applies to you?

Your dream about the future and all the good things it may hold for you pleases God, yet he asks you to do more than simply sit and expect a positive outcome. He delights to see you involved in working toward your great tomorrow by doing today whatever supports your purpose and brings your hopes and dreams to fruition. All the while, God supports you by assuring you of his excellent plans for you, his constant presence, and his unconditional love.

The eyes of all look expectantly to You. . . . You open Your hand and satisfy the desire of every living thing.

Psalm 145:15–16 NKJV

Heavenly Father: Hold me in your strong arms as I put my godly expectations into practice in productive and purposeful ways. Amen.

January 31

SPIRITUAL SAVVY

*See that you go on growing in the Lord, and become strong and
vigorous in the truth you were taught.*

Colossians 2:7 TLB

To grow physically, the body needs the right kind of food.
The same can be said for spiritual growth.

God provides just the right spiritual diet through the wisdom
and promises of the Bible. He spreads out a banquet in front of you
and says, "Come and eat of my comfort, peace, and love. Taste
what I have to offer." When you do, your spirit grows in knowledge
and understanding. Your spirit gains the
strength, energy, and vitality God intends
for you.

*Thank you, God,
for the spiritual
nourishment of the
Bible and for all the
ways I can exercise
my spirit in my
daily life. Amen.*

Accept God's invitation. Sit down to
feast at his banquet every day. It will keep
your spirit growing and sustained.

Like newborn babies, long for the pure milk
of the word, so that by it you may grow.

1 Peter 2:2 NASB

FEBRUARY

*Whatever you do
in word or deed, do all in the
name of the Lord Jesus,
giving thanks through Him
to God the Father.*

COLOSSIANS 3:17 NASB

PRAISE TO THE END

Praise the Lord! Praise God in his sanctuary; praise him in his mighty heaven! Praise him for his mighty works; praise his unequaled greatness!

Psalm 150:1–2 NLT

he book of Psalms begins: "Happy are those who . . . love the Lord's teachings" (1:1–2 NCV), and ends: "Praise the Lord!" (150:6 NCV). In between is every situation you might experience on the journey of life—trials, losses, betrayals, joys, hopes, promises, and desires. The Psalms represent the whole spectrum of human experiences, and the faithfulness of God to walk with you through each one.

How blessed and fitting to praise you, God! May my life be a psalm of adoration to you from this time forth and forevermore. I'll love you always, my God. Amen.

Hopefully you have not missed this precious truth: When you begin with faith in God—reading the Bible and trusting his love—you end with praise for him.

So adore him! Worship him! Express your love for him from the depths of your soul! Because he will never let you down, and surely he is worthy.

Let everything that has breath praise the Lord. Praise the Lord.

Psalm 150:6 NIV

February 2

HE KEEPS HIS
PROMISES

No, I will not break my covenant; I will not take back a single word I said.

Psalm 89:34 NLT

One of the deepest hurts you can experience is betrayal. Discovering that a friend, co-worker, or loved one has acted treacherously can tempt you to feel defeated and rejected. Imagine what Jesus felt when he saw Judas walking toward him that night in the garden of Gethsemane.

Yet you can know that God would never betray your trust by breaking his promises to you. Not only would it contradict his holy character, it would violate his perfect love for you.

Is there some precious promise that is long in being fulfilled? God has not forgotten his word to you. On the contrary, what

> *God, it is very difficult to wait for my dreams and hopes to come to fruition. Yet I have confidence that you will keep all your promises to me. Amen.*

he is providing is too wonderful to create quickly. Therefore, wait upon him with confidence and hope, because he would never betray your trust.

Lord God of Hosts, who is strong like You, Lord? Your faithfulness surrounds You.

Psalm 89:8 HCSB

An Attitude of Adoration

*It is good to give thanks to the Lord, to sing praises to your name,
O Most High; to declare your steadfast love in the morning, and
your faithfulness by night.*

Psalm 92:1–2 ESV

Battling difficulties can be draining and may alter the way you view your circumstances. Instead of seeing the potential of your life, you begin to feel that you are not special and that God has forgotten you. His good plan for your life seems more and more unlikely every time you think about it.

However, remember that his goal for you is always geared for ultimate victory and success. Therefore, the best remedy for your heart is to sing songs of praise to remind you of his goodness.

No matter what you are facing, God will lift your spirit when you worship him. This is what the psalmist did, which is why he wrote confidently and with great joy, "It is good to give thanks to the Lord."

God, you are my salvation and my source of joy and gladness. Truly it is good to praise you; and no matter what happens, I'll rejoice in your love for me! Amen.

You, O Lord, have made me glad by what You have done, I will sing for joy at the works of Your hands.

Psalm 92:4 NASB

February 4

JOY TO SHARE

Celebrate God all day, every day. I mean, revel in him!
Philippians 4:4 THE MESSAGE

Throughout these pages, you have reflected on many aspects of the Christian journey, and now God's Spirit invites you to receive a gift for every step along the way—joy so abundant you cannot contain it within yourself.

God-given joy overflows your heart and shows in your appreciation for life, your gratitude for God's blessings, and your trust in his forgiveness, protection, and care. In the things you do and say each day, the joy of your heart shines through to others, and the serenity of your soul touches the world with his peace.

Open your arms and lavish others with your gift of abundant joy.

Yes, the Lord has done amazing things for us! What joy!

Psalm 126:3 NLT

Heavenly Father:
Lead me to receive
your precious gift with
gratitude, sharing
the riches of your joy
with others as you
so graciously share
yourself with me.
Amen.

TO THE FINISH

When your endurance is fully developed, you will be perfect and complete, needing nothing.

James 1:4 NLT

ecause she wanted to enter a marathon, a woman spent several months in training. Each day she ran a little farther until she could run the full distance, and on race day she ran the race to the finish.

The Christian life can be compared to a race, because living it requires daily determination to build the spiritual strength required to complete the long course ahead. The energy and effort you put into pursuing godly goals will reward you with the gifts of determination, fortitude, and satisfaction.

When challenges come, remember this: God has promised to see you through to the finish, but you must be prepared.

O God: Create in me a spirit of determination, strength, and stamina so I may remain surely and steadily on your path. I want to run to the finish. Amen.

Let us run with endurance the race God has set before us.

Hebrews 12:1 NLT

A WELCOME PURSUIT

Those who know your name will trust in you, for you, Lord, have never forsaken those who seek you.

Psalm 9:10 NIV

Chase fame, power, accomplishments, or social status, and you may discover that the more you have, the more unstable you feel. Try to fill your innermost needs with wealth, relationships, or activities, and you will probably find yourself with a greater sense of dissatisfaction than you have ever felt before. Attempt to escape your sorrows with food, alcohol, or other substances, and the gnawing emptiness within you will only increase.

God, I want to know you more — teach me your ways. Thank you that when I seek you, I find everything I need and all that my heart desires. Amen.

Yet pursue God, and the doors of joy and fulfillment will spring open. Not only does he give you a firm place to stand and satisfy your soul but he also fills your life with his presence, love, and purpose. Seek him with all of your heart, therefore, because you will certainly find what you are looking for.

The Lord has made Himself known.

Psalm 9:16 NASB

CONGRATULATIONS IN ORDER

The humble will see their God at work and be glad.

Psalm 69:32 NLT

To avoid the appearance of bragging, many of us keep quiet about our successes and accomplishments. Such modesty, however, robs us of the joy of sharing our happiness, and takes from others the chance to offer their congratulations and praise.

Dear God: Thank you for giving me many reasons to celebrate. Let me use each occasion to spread the word of your wonderful ways. Amen.

Your successes are an opportunity to invite friends to celebrate with you, giving thanks to God for his goodness in your life. Your joy may prompt them to reflect on his work in their lives, an opening God's Spirit may use to draw them closer to him and strengthen their faith.

When you have reason to celebrate, share the news about what God has done through you and rejoice with others.

A cheerful look brings joy to the heart; good news makes for good health.

Proverbs 15:30 NLT

February 8

FIRST PLACE

Seek the Kingdom of God above all else, and live righteously, and he will give you everything you need.

Matthew 6:33 NLT

Many women say they cherish the time they spend in prayer during the quiet hours of the early morning. In a truly physical way, they're giving God first place in their day.

Getting up before dawn may not work for you, but putting God first in your thoughts, words, and actions yields extraordinary rewards. You move with God-given purpose, and you gain peace of mind knowing you're doing the right thing for the right reasons. Among the options available to you, choose those things poised to enrich your life and the lives of those around you.

All times of day (or night), let God come first in your life.

Seek those things which are above, where Christ is, sitting at the right hand of God.

Colossians 3:1 NKJV

Dear God: Grant me the willingness and the courage to give you first place in my thoughts, words, and actions. Amen.

A SOLID PLACE
TO STAND

From the end of the earth I will cry to You, when my heart is overwhelmed; lead me to the rock that is higher than I.

Psalm 61:2 NKJV

At times you may lose your perspective about a situation because it is so overwhelming and earth-shattering. Perhaps you have done something that cannot be fixed, and the realization of your mistake is taking you on a downward spiral of disappointment. God knows your heart, and he is willing to come to your aid.

On several occasions, David's confidence was shaken by his enemies, but the Lord repeatedly sustained him and gave him the victory. No matter what happened, he learned that God was with him, and that reality gave him peace.

Is your world being shaken by a tremendous challenge? Experiencing God's presence provided David with the stability and strength he needed to continue, and the same can be true for you. Therefore, plant your hope firmly in him.

God, please help me to sense your presence and rest in your care. Thank you for giving me a solid place to stand though the world around me quakes. Amen.

You have been a refuge for me, a strong tower in the face of the enemy. I will live in Your tent forever and take refuge under the shelter of Your wings.

Psalm 61:3–4 HCSB

TRANQUIL WATERS

*O Lord, you will ordain peace for us, for indeed, all that we
have done, you have done for us.*

Isaiah 26:12 NRSV

If you're like most women, you fill many roles.
Pressure can arise when these roles conflict, and
sometimes it can be overwhelming and plunge you into a sea
of stress. God understands the agony of stress, and he provides
relief for its presence in your life.

God says, "Bring your troubles to me and leave them with
me." He knows the burden you're carrying can be too heavy and
hard for you to bear. Once you let him lift the weight from your
shoulders, stress washes away from your body and spirit.

Open yourself to God's peace and rest
in the tranquil and rejuvenating waters of
his care for you.

Cast all your anxiety on him because he
cares for you.

1 Peter 5:7 NIV

*O God: I rely on your
divine strength. Let me
give to you the burdens
of my heart. Provide
for me your soothing,
rejuvenating rest.
Amen.*

THEN I AM STRONG

When I am weak [in human strength], then am I [truly] strong (able, powerful in divine strength).

2 Corinthians 12:10 AMP

*Y*ou know your weaknesses—and perhaps you regret them. However, they are the very areas through which God can perform miraculously.

Conversely, when you have exceptional talents and assets, you can fall into the trap of thinking you do not need God.

God, I praise you for my weaknesses. Thank you for achieving your great plans and showing me your glory through them. Amen.

Though he can work through you when you acknowledge you need him, it is a different story when you believe you can accomplish everything by yourself. Then he must teach you that his good plans are achieved only through his power—which is far greater than yours.

So don't worry about your weaknesses today—they are blessings in disguise. They are wonderful opportunities for God to show you his glory.

If I must boast, I would rather boast about the things that show how weak I am. God, the Father of our Lord Jesus, who is to be praised forever, knows I tell the truth.

2 Corinthians 11:30–31 NLT

WORSHIPING TOGETHER

I was glad when they said to me, "Let us go to the house of the Lord."

Psalm 122:1 NASB

Why is it important to go to church—to worship and serve God with other believers? It is important because you were created for deep fellowship with God and with his people.

Unfortunately, sometimes we think that "church" is merely singing a few hymns and listening to a sermon. Although that is part of it, what's missing is how you discover and implement God's purpose for your life in partnership with those who will love, encourage, and equip you. It is in relationship with other believers that God helps you become all you were created to be.

Church isn't a country club for Christians; it is a living community that exists to edify its members and glorify God. Don't avoid it! Join your brothers and sisters in Christ, and worship him together as you were created to.

> Because of my friends and my relatives, I will pray for peace. And because of the house of the Lord our God, I will work for your good.

Psalm 122:8–9 CEV

God, I thank you for the church—for sisters and brothers to share with, learn from, relate to, and depend upon. Develop your love for the church within me. Amen.

February 13

DECEPTIVE FEELINGS

O Lord, why do you stand so far away? Why do you hide when I am in trouble?

Psalm 10:1 NLT

he circumstances that trouble you may suggest that God has abandoned you. Yet the truth is, he will never leave you or forsake you. It may seem as if God is ignoring your prayers and tears, but he takes special care of each one. Your heart may even cry out, "My God, why don't you help me?" However, he is working all things out for your good even when you cannot see it.

At times your feelings will tempt you to doubt God, which is why you must always cling to the promises he gives you in his Word. Never allow your emotions to cloud the truth of God's unfailing love. The fact is, he is with you and will never fail you. Therefore, rejoice in his holy name.

God, I praise you for sticking by me —even when my heart begins to wander. Please forgive me for doubting you. Help me to trust you more. Amen.

Lord, surely you see these cruel and evil things. People in trouble look to you for help. You are the one who helps the orphans.

Psalm 10:14 NCV

WHAT GOES AROUND

Always try to do good to each other.
1 Thessalonians 5:15 NLT

ave you noticed it is often easier to extend kindness to others than to accept kindness? You've been sick for days and a friend offers to bring you some warm, nourishing comfort food. But you say, "Oh no, I'm fine." In your effort not to inconvenience the other person, you block the blessing such kindness can bring for both of you.

God often chooses to love and care for us through others, so be quick to receive the loving care he offers and be grateful for the hands that bring it. You can be sure that he blesses them richly for their trouble. Always say yes to a kindness extended.

> Be kindly affectionate to one another with brotherly love, in honor giving preference to one another.
>
> Romans 12:10 NKJV

Dear God: In your Spirit, enable me to freely receive the kindnesses others extend, remembering that they will be blessed as well. Amen.

February 15

YESTERDAY, TODAY, AND FOREVER

Your throne, O Lord, has stood from time immemorial. You yourself are from the everlasting past.

Psalm 93:2 NLT

When you acknowledge God's power and might, he pours his encouragement into your heart. A simple prayer, "Lord, I need your help," speaks volumes to him. He hears your confession and moves into action.

Yet there will be times when you do not have days or weeks to pray about what you are facing. An emergency will arise, and within a few minutes or even seconds, you will need his comfort and direction. Can God help you in such urgent situations?

Yes, he is perfectly able to provide all you need the moment you cry out to him.

So take heart, friend, in your faithful God. He is as faithful to you today as he has been from time immemorial. And he will surely come to your aid as soon as you call.

God, you are truly faithful—as you were yesterday, you will be today and forevermore. Thank you that I can always trust your mighty, loving hand. Amen.

Lord, your laws will stand forever. Your Temple will be holy forevermore.

Psalm 93:5 NCV

THINGS COULD
BE WORSE

What if the Lord had not been on our side?
Psalm 124:1 GNT

*I*t happens without fail. Some extra money comes your way, and you know just what to do with it. Then your car breaks down. There goes your bonus. Or you finally take a day off work, and you look forward to relaxing. Then a loved one has an emergency. There goes your vacation.

In a sense, you may feel as if you were robbed of a blessing. However, what you need to remember is that things could have been much worse. Imagine not having the money to pay for that repair, or taking that loved one to the doctor during high-pressure deadlines.

You had other plans, but God was providing for what he knew was ahead. Therefore, embrace it as a special blessing and praise him for helping you.

> *God, please forgive me when I have a bad attitude. Thank you so much for providing for me. I don't know what I would do without your wonderful grace! Amen.*

Blessed be God! He didn't go off and leave us. He didn't abandon us defenseless. . . . God's strong name is our help, the same God who made heaven and earth.

Psalm 124:6, 8 THE MESSAGE

February 17

FROM ETERNITY

From everlasting to everlasting, You are God. . . . For a thousand years in Your sight are like yesterday when it passes by.

Psalm 90:2, 4 NASB

There is no one like the Lord God. Nothing on this earth compares to his greatness. He can easily deal with the ongoing operation of the universe, and at the same time be intimately interested in every detail of your day—no matter how great or small it may be.

God knew you before he formed the foundation of the earth. He is omniscient—he knows the desires of your heart and the prayers you will pray even before you lift your eyes to heaven in hopeful expectation of his answer.

As you begin your day and before you turn your light out at night, take time to thank him for caring for you so dearly and completely. His love for you is from everlasting, so make sure you praise his wonderful name.

Lord, you set the heavens in place and know every star that shines. Yet you also know the slightest detail of my life and I praise you for your care. Amen.

Teach us to number our days aright, that we may gain a heart of wisdom. . . . Satisfy us in the morning with your unfailing love, that we may sing for joy and be glad all our days.

Psalm 90:12, 14 NIV

EVERYDAY CHOICES

Choose life, that both you and your descendants may live.

Deuteronomy 30:19 NKJV

Most of us spend time thinking and weighing options before making important decisions, but we often forget the significance of choices we make every day—our words, our actions and reactions, our attitude and our outlook.

Consider God's life-giving choices. His compassion shines in you when you opt for the gentle word and kindly gesture, even when tempers flare. His effective work is reflected in your productive choices, those choices that build up and bring about positive change, and his peace flows through your faithful efforts to maintain harmony between yourself and others.

> *Dear God: As you have chosen me to follow you, help me make godly and life-affirming decisions and choices in all I do each day. Amen.*

God's presence shows when your small, everyday choices reflect his Spirit's work in your heart.

I bless the Lord who gives me counsel.

Psalm 16:7 NRSV

GOOD WORK

Enjoy the work you do here on earth. Whatever work you do, do your best.

Ecclesiastes 9:9–10 NCV

A routine transaction with a woman occupying a low-paying position leaves you uplifted and inspired. Why? Because she performed her job with dignity, grace, and generosity of spirit, and she obviously cared about her work. You think, "If she can find satisfaction in her work, why can't I in mine?"

Dear God: Grant me a spirit of joy in doing the work that lies before me each day. In you I find my inspiration. Amen.

Similar incidents happen in all walks of life, and each shows how attitude more than circumstance determines how you feel about yourself and your work. Your willingness to do your best at whatever the day brings and seek the good in whatever situation you find yourself identifies you as a joyful woman of noble and godly character.

All to whom God gives wealth and possessions and whom he enables to enjoy them, and to accept their lot and find enjoyment in their toil—this is the gift of God.

Ecclesiastes 5:19 NRSV

A DAILY NEED

For God alone, O my soul, wait in silence, for my hope is from him. He only is my rock and my salvation, my fortress; I shall not be shaken.

Psalm 62:5–6 ESV

Every day, you will face challenges—some of them are simple to solve, while others are more trying. There will be times when you will want to rush ahead of God, even though you do not have a clear plan.

However, he is allowed that difficulty so that you will learn to trust him at a deeper level—seeking him consistently for your needs. His timing in your situation is perfect, and if you move too quickly, you risk missing his best.

If you seek him daily and wait for him to work on your behalf, you will discover that your waiting is not in vain. Therefore, when trouble comes, ask him to show you how to deal with the matter and allow him to draw you even closer through it.

God, teach me to wait for your very best and to rest in the safety of your care. Every day I will seek your face and trust you to lead me. Amen.

Trust God, my friends, and always tell him each one of your concerns. God is our place of safety.

Psalm 62:8 CEV

February 21

THE GREATEST LOVE OF ALL

Yes, I have loved you with an everlasting love.

Jeremiah 31:3 NKJV

Think about what you love most in the world. Now try to multiply that love by infinity. The human mind cannot contain such a concept. In the same way, we cannot even begin to comprehend the magnitude of God's love for us. It's a love that will last forever, and it remains unchanged in the face of our mistakes, unaltered by time or circumstances.

You have probably been looking for such a love all your life. You may think you don't deserve to be loved so deeply and unconditionally. The fact is that God's love is not limited by our small thinking. God, who knows you best, loves you most.

*Heavenly Father:
I can't comprehend
the depths of your love
for me. But I receive it
with a grateful heart.
Amen.*

How precious is Your lovingkindness, O God!
    And the children of men take refuge in the shadow of Your wings.

Psalm 36:7 NASB

A HEAVENLY PERSPECTIVE

The Lord is in his holy temple; the Lord is on his heavenly throne.
He observes the sons of men; his eyes examine them.

Psalm 11:4 NIV

Is safety important to you? Would you like to feel secure in your home, finances, relationships, and occupation? Are you ever afraid of the future—of being unprepared for the challenges ahead?

Fears about the unknown can steal your peace. Yet understand that although your perspective is limited, God's is not. That is why your best safeguard is always to trust him.

From his heavenly throne, God sees the troubles on the path before you, and he can lead you through them unharmed. He also examines the dangers within you—the harmful behaviors that undermine your life—and frees you from them.

God, you know my fears and my need for security. Help me to trust and obey you so that I can remain in the center of your perfect care. Amen.

Therefore, be confident in God's unfailing perspective and discover real security in your relationship with him. There is no safer place to be than in his wonderful care.

I trust in the Lord for protection.

Psalm 11:1 NCV

February 23

SHARE A PRAYER

While they are still talking about their needs, I will go ahead and answer their prayers!

Isaiah 65:24 NLT

The telephone rang. "I'm calling to ask for your prayers," the caller said, then proceeded to explain that the husband of a co-worker was undergoing surgery.

God offers you the privilege and the power to pray for the needs of your family, friends, and associates, in addition to the needs of individuals or groups brought to your attention by word of mouth or through the media.

Heavenly Father: I come before you with the needs of others on my heart, and I pray you will look compassionately on them and console them in their distress. Amen.

Share your prayers by pleading the cause of others, and let the sound of your voice come before the throne of God your heavenly Father, who has promised to hear the prayers of every believing heart.

"Call to me in times of trouble, I will save you and you will honor me," [declares the Lord].

Psalm 50:15 NCV

February 24

JUSTICE SERVED

The godly will rejoice when they see injustice avenged.
Psalm 58:10 NLT

oes it ever seem as if the unrighteous get away with their terrible schemes, while you are always caught no matter what mistake you make?

The truth is, no one really gets away with anything. Sin has many consequences, and God holds each person accountable for his or her actions. However, he does not want you dwelling on how and when he will move against the unjust. Rather, he calls you to be mindful of his ability to deal with every situation. He is in control, and in his perfect timing every wrong will be addressed.

God, teach me to pray for those who do not know you and to act wisely as I live my life for you. I praise you for righting every wrong. Amen.

He also wants you to pray for those who are trapped in sin—because it is only when they know him that they will be able to escape from its terrible grasp.

Everyone will say, "It's true! Good people are rewarded. God does rule the earth with justice."

Psalm 58:11 CEV

CELEBRATION OF BLESSINGS

The faithful will abound with blessings.
Proverbs 28:20 NRSV

When we are hesitant to join with others in joyful celebration of God's blessings, we are like the wallflower at the dance, too shy to step out of the shadows onto the dance floor.

At every stage of your life, you have been given unique and personal blessings by your heavenly Father, blessings he intends that you recognize and use to benefit yourself and others. If you hold the blessing of a positive outlook, share hope; if good health, share help; if intelligence, share insight; if curiosity, discover more about God's goodness and tell others what you found.

Celebrate your blessings by stepping out of the shadows and sharing with others.

Blessed shall you be when you come in, and blessed shall you be when you go out.
Deuteronomy 28:6 NASB

Dear God: I come to you in humble thanks for the blessings I have received. Teach me how to share with others your goodness to me. Amen.

February 26

TO THE FINISH

You need to persevere so that when you have done the will of God, you will receive what he has promised.

Hebrews 10:36 NIV

Think of a time you continued with a difficult task until you completed it. In all likelihood, you determined to see it through because you kept a goal in mind—a good grade, praise, or simply the satisfaction of a job well done. Your perseverance had a reward.

Your growth in God is a lifelong project, and God has put a goal in front of you to encourage you to carry it to the finish. He assures you of everlasting life with him and the reward of his approval. His promises not only offer you hope for today but show you the heavenly result of remaining faithful to him.

Dear God: When the way you have prepared for me seems difficult, remind me of the blessings you have in store for those who persevere to the end. Amen.

[Jesus said,] "I'll make each conqueror a pillar in the sanctuary of my God, a permanent position of honor.

Revelation 3:12 THE MESSAGE

February 27

MANY HANDS, LIGHT WORK

Be strong and do not lose courage, for there is reward for your work.

2 Chronicles 15:7 NASB

sk for volunteers, and the same hands go up every time! Consider volunteering when work needs to get done, even if you normally don't volunteer.

You have specific skills and special know-how needed in your home, at your workplace, in your community, and God calls you to willingly and gladly share your expertise with others. When you take on any task within your power to perform, you not only lighten the load for others who help, you receive the satisfaction of sharing your abilities, and serve as a compelling example for women who do not yet know the joy of responding to a call for help.

Dear God: Increase in me the desire to share my skills with others, and grant me a willingness to step forward to help in whatever way I can. Amen.

My heart took delight in all my work, and this was the reward for all my labor.

Ecclesiastes 2:10 NIV

AVAILABLE

My eyes are weak from crying. Lord, I have prayed to you every day; I have lifted my hands in prayer to you.

Psalm 88:9 NCV

Disappointment can strike suddenly and your first reaction may be one of defensiveness. You may feel angry and hurt; however, do not lash out. Your best course of action is always to step away from the situation and ask God to show you what to do.

The wonderful thing about God is that he is always accessible and willing to receive you. He will show you what you need to do and comfort your aching heart.

Has discouragement assailed you? Are your eyes weak from crying and your heart tender and grieved? God will find a way to encourage you and admonish you not to give up. So turn to him—because even at this moment, he is listening for your call.

I know that when I keep my eyes on you, Lord, you will give me the comfort, the strength, and the understanding I need. Thank you for your unfailing love. Amen.

Lord, God of my salvation, I cry out before You day and night. May my prayer reach Your presence; listen to my cry.

Psalm 88:1–2 HCSB

MARCH

May the Lord be good to you

and give you peace.

NUMBERS 6:26 CEV

March 1

DISCERNMENT

Lord, save me from liars and from those who plan evil.
Psalm 120:2 NCV

Not all the blessings God sends your way are material in nature. In fact, one of the greatest blessings he gives is a spirit of discernment. This one gift will help you make wise choices at every turn.

Of course, you may wonder, *How do I gain this wonderful gift?* You begin by spending time with God in prayer and the study of the Bible.

The more you know about him, the more you will understand his ways, desires, and plans. He also will open your eyes so you're prepared for the challenges that come your way.

God, open my eyes so I can see what is right and true according to your principles. I don't desire worldly wisdom. I desire your truth for my life. Amen.

When you have his discernment, you have a greater sense of confidence and hope because you know that God is sovereign—ready, willing, and able to reveal his will to you and protect you in every situation.

In my distress I cried to the Lord, and He answered me.

Psalm 120:1 AMP

A PERSON HE LOVES

Great is His faithful love to us.
Psalm 117:2 HCSB

You don't need to worry about the future. God is in control and he will provide his very best for you—a daughter he loves dearly. He knows what you will face today, tomorrow, and forever, and how you should navigate through every twist and turn that life holds. He has a wonderful plan for you, but you must accept it.

You do so by asking him to keep you in the center of his will, and trusting him as he trains you to see your life and circumstances from his loving perspective.

While problems that stretch your faith will come, you can learn to look beyond them to when God triumphantly fulfills his purpose for your life and lovingly blesses you with his great and precious promises. Truly, you will never regret trusting him.

> Praise the Lord, all you nations! Praise him, all you people of the world!
>
> Psalm 117:1 GOD'S WORD

God, teach me to be still before you and wait for your leading before I move forward. I know it is in times of quiet that you whisper truth to my heart. Amen.

TIMELY MATTER

A wise heart knows the proper time and procedure. For there is a proper time and procedure for every delight.

Ecclesiastes 8:5–6 NASB

As we mature, we come to realize how quickly days melt into years. We recognize time as our most precious gift—the gift God tells us to willingly and generously share with others.

The hours you spend taking care of your family, working to provide for them, visiting the sick, comforting your friends, and helping the needy please your heavenly Father. He delights when you take time for yourself to rest and be revived in him, to keep your spiritual fire burning inside.

Dear God: Thank you for the days and years of my life. Bless the time I share with others so it will bring about happiness, encouragement, and peace. Amen.

God-pleasing and productive sharing won't slow down the passage of time, but it will lift up your spirits and leave you with a treasure chest of heartwarming memories.

Behold, now is the accepted time; behold, now is the day of salvation.

2 Corinthians 6:2 NKJV

STRONG WORDS

Deep in your hearts you know that every promise of the Lord your God has come true. Not a single one has failed!

Joshua 23:14 NLT

*Y*ou have my word on it." In big matters as in small, the phrase signals an intention to follow through on a promise given, an objective stated.

Being true to your word is a God-pleasing and Godlike attribute. It's God-pleasing because constancy builds trust between you and others and enhances your reputation as a woman who does what she says she will do. It's Godlike because God is true to his Word, and in his Word he has declared to you his eternal love. Even if you falter in your promises, God remains unwavering in his promise to care for you. You have his Word on it.

Never let go of loyalty and faithfulness.

Proverbs 3:3 GNT

Dear God: Your infinite and steadfast fidelity fills my heart with gratitude. Keep me firm in my faithfulness to the promises I make to others. Amen.

HAPPINESS FOR A LIFETIME

God gives wisdom, knowledge, and joy to those who please him.

Ecclesiastes 2:26 NLT

As you turn your thoughts to God, you realize more and more that the happiness the world brings you creates temporary contentment, at best.

God intends for you to have a lifetime of happiness, so he has sent his Spirit to live in your heart. His Spirit produces joy, an inner joy neither dampened nor discouraged by outward events and circumstances. Assured that you belong to God, with your reliance firmly planted in his strength and your trust resolutely set on his promises, you can take hold of genuine happiness.

It's free, it comes from God, and it's yours to keep forever.

Heavenly Father: Grant me the courage to reach out and take hold of the joy you have in store for me, because I desire a joyful heart and happy spirit. Amen.

I will greatly rejoice in the Lord, my soul shall be joyful in my God.

Isaiah 61:10 NKJV

GODLY LOVE

Live a life of love, just as Christ loved us and gave himself up for us as a fragrant offering and sacrifice to God.

Ephesians 5:2 NIV

hen we speak with one another about love, we're often talking about sex, or emotions and feelings. When God talks about love, he has in mind a far more powerful, more encompassing, more lasting kind of love.

Biblical love reflects God's attitude toward you, a disposition rooted in his selfless decision to be and remain in love with you. His unchangeable feelings for you mean your relationship with him is one of eternal stability, and his love a worthy dwelling place for your feelings of gratitude, joy, and love.

Dear God: As I become more aware of your feelings toward me, allow your committed and selfless love to permeate all my relationships. Amen.

In his eternal embrace, you know true love, and God invites you to share his attitude of love with others.

Blessed be the Lord, for he has wondrously shown his steadfast love to me.

Psalm 31:21 NRSV

HE PREFERS YOUR TRUST

The Lord takes pleasure in those who reverently and worshipfully fear Him, in those who hope in His mercy and loving-kindness.

Psalm 147:11 AMP

It is easy to be stuck on a certain idea of what the Christian life should be. Going to church, reading your Bible, having a prayer time—it becomes a burdensome routine. Somehow, God is left out.

However, the purpose for fellowshipping with other believers, studying the Bible, and praying should be so you can know him better—not so you can check off a list of what it means to be a "good Christian."

God wants a living, growing, personal relationship with you that leads to loving obedience, not meaningless ritual. He wants your trust.

So be willing to give up your religious practices and pursue a deep relationship with God. Then you won't just have an idea of the Christian life—you'll be experiencing it abundantly.

God, I want to know you in an authentic, profound relationship. Teach me to have full confidence in you, my God, for you are surely worthy of all my trust. Amen.

How good it is to sing praises to our God, how pleasant and fitting to praise him! . . . Great is our Lord and mighty in power; his understanding has no limit.

Psalm 147:1, 5 NIV

GRACE AND DISGRACE

When pride comes, then comes dishonor, but with the humble is wisdom.

Proverbs 11:2 NASB

*P*ride poses as our friend, but it is our enemy. Pride moves us into a place where we don't belong. And sooner or later God has no other choice. Like a security officer who escorts a trespasser from the stage at a concert, God must remove us from that place of pretending and put us where we do belong.

The humble need not fear this. They won't lose face because they don't need to put on airs. They don't need to pretend. They derive their value and significance from God rather than from an exaggerated sense of their own self-importance.

You will sidestep the trap of pride by putting God and others first.

> *God, save me from the trap of pride. I want to put you and others first. Please show me how today. Amen.*

Human pride will be brought down, and human arrogance will be humbled. Only the Lord will be exalted on that day of judgment.

Isaiah 2:11 NLT

UNTIL YOUR SOUL IS SATISFIED

O God, you are my God, and I long for you. My whole being desires you; like a dry, worn-out, and waterless land, my soul is thirsty for you.

Psalm 63:1 GNT

Responsibilities and struggles can drain your energy and emotions. Trials threaten to steal your hope and joy. You survey the circumstances of your life and wonder how any good can come from what you are experiencing. But it can. When God is involved, there is always the potential for hope and blessing.

God, thank you for inviting me to experience your wonderful love. I long to know you better and experience your encouraging, satisfying presence. Amen.

Problems are a natural part of life. Without much warning, stress can build, and before you know it, you are crying out for help. However, instead of cowering in fear, the psalmist used his trying situation as an opportunity to express his deep commitment to God.

Can you? Have you found shelter in the Lord's presence and fulfillment in his love? Then praise him for satisfying your hungry, weary soul, and express your trust that he will work everything out for your good.

You satisfy me more than the richest feast. I will praise you with songs of joy.

Psalm 63:5 NLT

THE COMING RESCUE

"Because of the oppression of the weak and the groaning of the needy, I will now arise," says the Lord. "I will protect them from those who malign them."

Psalm 12:5 NIV

When David faced Goliath, he was merely a boy and was unfamiliar with the sword. One might imagine that David was afraid to face the massive giant. After all, everyone else in Israel was. Yet instead of being frightened by Goliath's threats, David remembered the faithfulness of God, and he trusted the Lord to rescue him.

God, no challenge is too difficult for you! Thank you for giving me hope in this trial. I know I am never alone or defeated as long as you're with me. Amen.

Are you on your own to face a challenge that is too enormous to handle? Are the negative comments of others filling you with fear and discouragement? Call out to God, and obey whatever he tells you. Just as he rescued David by empowering him to slay Goliath, he will give you triumph over your trial if you will trust him. So do not fear. Your deliverance is coming. Watch for it.

The words of the Lord are pure words, like silver tried in a furnace of earth, purified seven times.

Psalm 12:6 NKJV

A CLEAR CONSCIENCE

I try my best to have a clear conscience in whatever I do for God or for people.

Acts 24:16 CEV

*R*egret-free living starts with a clear conscience. Making the hard choice to do what is right today frees you from sleepless nights tomorrow. Righteous living keeps you from needing to cover your tracks with lies and releases you from that sick feeling of guilt inside.

God, I want to live without guilt. Please meet me in those places where I struggle so that temptations lose their power. Amen.

You know this instinctively. And you maintain a clear conscience by inviting God into those places in your heart that contain your struggles, your dreams, your temptations, your fears, and your desires. As you relate to God on this intimate level, you delight in knowing that God has your best interests in mind when he lays down the standards of conduct you are to follow.

Let's come near God with pure hearts and a confidence that comes from having faith. Let's keep our hearts pure, our consciences free from evil.

Hebrews 10:22 CEV

TRUE POSSESSING

[Jesus said,] "Live generously and graciously toward others, the way God lives toward you."

Matthew 5:48 THE MESSAGE

"Here, use mine for as long as you need it," she said, handing her roommate a coat from her closet. She knew a tight budget restricted her roommate's spending, and the coat would get her through the winter.

Sharing comes naturally when you recognize your possessions belong not to you but to God. He has graciously given them to you to use and enjoy, and he delights to see your pleasure in sharing what you have with others. In doing so, you develop generosity and prevent your possessions from possessing you. You also become a partner with God by helping him answer someone else's prayer and fill someone else's need.

[God] will make you rich in every way so that you can always give freely.

2 Corinthians 9:11 NCV

Heavenly Father: All I have comes from you. Help me develop a spirit of generosity and sharing with others so I may become more like you. Amen.

ONE STORY

You shall know the truth, and the truth shall make you free.

John 8:32 NKJV

magine hearing a story from one friend, then hearing a different account from another friend. You realize because you didn't witness the actual event, you may never know what really happened.

God understands the limitations of human reason and experience, and has given you a way to know the facts of his work on Earth, his love for you, and his promise of heaven. He provides the Bible as a means of opening spiritual truths to you. As you read or hear it, his Spirit informs your heart and mind of facts you can discover no other way than through his Word.

With God, you have one story—the true story.

Heavenly Father: Turn my attention to you and your Word as I search for the truth about you and your ways among people and in my own life. Amen.

Your lovingkindness is before my eyes, and I have walked in Your truth.

Psalm 26:3 NKJV

March 14

GOOD CHEER

Be made new in the attitude of your minds.
Ephesians 4:23 NIV

Martha Washington once said, "I've learned from experience that the greater part of our happiness or misery depends on our dispositions and not on our circumstances."

When you commit yourself to optimism, adverse circumstances shrink to their proper size. Your positive outlook enables you to see the best and make the best of situations. Good things begin to happen because of your constructive and purposeful thinking, words, and actions. You learn you can cope, and cope well and you find great and lasting pleasure in your God-given strengths and abilities.

A cheerful disposition looks at the world through the eyes of God's life-affirming goodness and love.

> Your attitude should be the kind that was shown us by Jesus Christ.
>
> Philippians 2:5 TLB

Dear God: Renew in me a godly attitude of optimism, and restore my mind with confidence in your willingness to see me through whatever comes my way in life. Amen.

OUTWARD ACTION

Serve wholeheartedly, as if you were serving the Lord, not men, because you know that the Lord will reward everyone for whatever good he does.

Ephesians 6:7–8 NIV

When you consider what you do each day, you might imagine you are limited in your ability to serve others. Not so!

God uses you to bring the reality of his presence wherever you are, and he offers you opportunities to act as his voice and his hands as you go about your daily tasks. When you speak affirming words and offer kindly help, and when you willingly step out to assist those in need or support worthy causes, you are serving others.

Take a moment to reflect on how you can serve others today, and you will find as many ways as there are godly thoughts, desires, words, and actions.

O God: Fill me with desire to serve others in the things I do and say: Open my eyes and heart to the opportunities before me today. Amen.

If anyone serves, he should do it with the strength God provides, so that in all things God may be praised through Jesus Christ.

1 Peter 4:11 NIV

ENCIRCLED BY STRENGTH

As the mountains surround Jerusalem, so the Lord surrounds His people from this time forth and forever.

Psalm 125:2 NKJV

he word *Jerusalem* may be translated "teaching or legacy of peace." Undoubtedly, the City of David was very tranquil when the psalmist lived there. Buttressed by Mounts Olivet and Scopus—as well as the valleys of Hinnom, Tyropoeon, and Kidron—Jerusalem was virtually inaccessible to invading armies. She was, indeed, a place of peace.

Sadly, enemies eventually found a way in—as is generally the case with any earthly defense. History bears witness that the tranquility that once characterized Jerusalem is no more.

Has this happened to you? Have your earthly defenses failed you? Remember, they are imperfect and may falter, but the living God is your true protection. He will teach your heart lasting peace that none can ever take away by, surrounding you with his love, wisdom, and strength from this time forth and forevermore.

God, you are and always will be my perfect Defender! I praise you for covering me with your wisdom, strength, and love. May you be exalted forever! Amen.

Those who trust the Lord are like Mount Zion, which can never be shaken. It remains firm forever.

Psalm 125:1 GOD'S WORD

*Do not be afraid of sudden panic,
or of the storm that strikes the wicked;
for the Lord will be your confidence.*

PROVERBS 3:25–26 NRSV

March 17

DISCIPLINE OF THE HEART

How blessed the man you train, God, the woman you instruct in your Word.

Psalm 94:12 THE MESSAGE

Have you ever considered whether you are a living reflection of God's mercy and grace to others? If not, then you should ask God to teach you how to be an instrument of his love and understanding.

Each day you must deal with all kinds of situations—such as rude store clerks who test your patience and irate drivers in traffic who make your blood boil. However, each of these is an opportunity for you to demonstrate your true character—to show what is really in your heart.

To react in a manner that honors God takes discipline. So the next time you are annoyed, angered, or aggravated, think of it as an opportunity to share his grace with the offender. Certainly God will bless your efforts to be more like him.

When I felt my feet slipping, you came with your love and kept me steady. And when I was burdened with worries, you comforted me and made me feel secure.

Psalm 94:18–19 CEV

God, there are times when I need a firm reminder that I belong to you and my actions reflect what is hidden in my heart. Please help me to honor you. Amen.

ONLY ONE WILL DO

You are great and do wondrous things; you alone are God. Teach me your way, O Lord, that I may walk in your truth; unite my heart to fear your name.

Psalm 86:10–11 ESV

t times you may be tempted to think that God is not intimately aware of the dreams you have for the future. But he is. He knows the deepest desires of your heart because he has placed many of them within you.

However, he will not compete with the desires of your heart—he wants to be your priority. If you place anything above him, he will remove it because only he deserves first place in your life.

Are the desires of your heart united to honor him? Or are they divided between him and some other person or object of desire? Remember that it is God who gives you life and everything you have, so honor him above all else. You may be very surprised by how he rewards your faithfulness.

> *God, I want you to be first in my life. Though it is painful, please remove anything that hinders me from honoring you first and foremost. Amen.*

> I will give thanks to you with all my heart, O Lord my God. I will honor you forever because your mercy toward me is great. You have rescued me from the depths of hell.
>
> Psalm 86:12–13 GOD'S WORD

March 19

GOD TALK

God abides in those who confess that Jesus is the Son of God, and they abide in God.

1 John 4:15 NRSV

One woman of faith concludes her e-mails with the words "Have a great day in Jesus." Another believing woman sprinkles her conversations with "God willing" and "Praise God!" These phrases invite God into the conversation and give joyful witness to his presence.

Dear God: Grant me boldness in speaking about you and the faith you have planted in my heart. I want to become a winsome witness to others. Amen.

Casual references to your faith in God give you opportunities to share your beliefs with another person, because his name coming reverently from your lips establishes you as either a fellow believer in whom another can confide, or a source of information for someone who has questions.

You naturally talk about what's important to you, and it's natural for you to talk about God.

You are the light of the world. . . . Let your light shine before others, so that they may see your good works and give glory to your Father in heaven.

Matthew 5:14, 16 NRSV

YIELDING TO TRUST

I was pushed back and about to fall, but the Lord helped me.

Psalm 118:13 NIV

ews of a sudden sorrow or a shift in the way you live life can cause you to feel shaken. You may wonder if you'll be able to make it through another day. Frustration, stress, and pressure can overwhelm you, but you don't have to yield to discouragement. The psalmist placed his trust in God and found the help that he needed. You can too.

It may be tempting to charge ahead in your thoughts and begin to consider all that you can do to make life easier and better. However, moving forward without God's guidance will bring you even more disappointment.

> *God, thank you for guiding and comforting me through every decision and distress. I acknowledge that the best plan for my life is yours — in your timing. Amen.*

The best way to proceed is to seek God's will. Listen to him and trust him to guide your every step, because you will surely enjoy his untold blessings.

> The Lord is my strength and my song; he has given me victory. Songs of joy and victory are sung in the camp of the godly. The strong right arm of the Lord has done glorious things!
>
> Psalm 118:14–15 NLT

THAT'S HIS JOB

How great is the love the Father has lavished on us, that we should be called children of God!

1 John 3:1 NIV

o you ever think about how much God loves you? Some people rarely take time to do this. They are burdened by their problems, stresses, and shortcomings. They tell themselves that if they lived a better life, God would love them more. This simply is not true!

God loves you with an undivided love. Nothing you do can cause him to care for you any more or less. Rather, he accepts you just the way you are and his ultimate goal is to build you up in his image.

God created you for a relationship with himself, and he gently and compassionately molds you into all you were created to be. Therefore, rejoice! Because he is establishing you by his loving hand and will shine through you with his everlasting love.

God, I'm humbled by the fact that you love me and that you have a plan for my future. Thank you for molding me in your image. Amen.

A woman who respects the Lord should be praised.

Proverbs 31:30 NCV

BOLD MOVE

The righteous are as bold as a lion.
Proverbs 28:1 NRSV

Our culture generally ascribes valor to men. God however, not only recognizes valor in women but insists that we demonstrate it.

Godly valor doesn't require you to growl like a lion, but to walk with the assurance of one confident in God's presence and power to make things work for you when you follow his lead. Your godly valor consists of the willingness to encourage goodness and purity in all matters, to remind others of God's all-encompassing love and universal truths, and to stand firm when someone snarls at you to back down from the righteous path.

Valor ranks as a trait highly becoming of you, a woman of God.

> When I called, you answered me; you made me bold and stouthearted.
>
> Psalm 138:3 NIV

Heavenly Father: Help me grow in boldness so I will be willing and able to act with godly valor in the face of fear and temptation. Amen.

INTERMINABLE?

How long, O Lord? Will you forget me forever? . . . Consider and answer me, O Lord my God.

Psalm 13:1, 3 ESV

After weeks, months, perhaps even years of waiting for the Lord to work in a certain situation, you may feel weary and your hope may be fading. Maybe you are wondering, *Why is God taking so long? Why isn't he answering my prayers? Will this ever end?*

Waiting is difficult, but it is also necessary because it builds your faith in him. That is because you resolve to trust him even when every circumstance tells you not to. God rewards you by fulfilling the desires of your heart in a way more wonderful than you ever thought possible.

Therefore, friend, do not be discouraged—your wait is not in vain. God's provision is coming, and when it does, you will truly have great reason to rejoice.

I've thrown myself headlong into your arms—I'm celebrating your rescue. I'm singing at the top of my lungs, I'm so full of answered prayers.

Psalm 13:5–6 THE MESSAGE

God, thank you for this encouragement — I know you have not forgotten me. Help me to wait patiently and expectantly for your answer to my prayers. Amen.

UPWARD ACTION

Since we are receiving a kingdom which cannot be shaken, let us have grace, by which we may serve God acceptably with reverence and godly fear.

Hebrews 12:28 NKJV

In a relationship, love expresses itself in acts of kindness, thoughtfulness, and devotion. The same holds true for the relationship between you and God.

In the Bible, Jesus asks you to love God with your whole being and to put him above everyone and everything else in your heart. When you do so, you will want to obey him by responding to his Word and acting on those things you know he requires of you, simply for the sake of pleasing him.

As you grow in love and service, cultivating and using the gifts God has given you, your relationship will show all the signs of genuine love.

Dear God: Grant that I may learn to love you more, grow in obedience, and use for your service the gifts you have given to me. Amen.

Jesus said: "My Father will honor the one who serves me."

John 12:26 NIV

HE IS YOUR JOY

Shout his praise with joy! For great is the Holy One of Israel who lives among you.

Isaiah 12:6 NLT

God does not dwell on your mistakes. Rather, he faithfully turns away from anger in order to comfort and heal you. You are his joy.

He saves you from traps and schemes. Always trustworthy, he chases away all of your fears. He is your protector, defender, redeemer, savior, and friend. You are his joy.

He satisfies the deepest hungers of your soul. He teaches your heart with wisdom and nourishes your soul with his presence. You are his joy.

So praise God today, for his goodness and might. Thank him that all your great blessings have come from his hand. Express your loving thoughts toward him—because he is *your* joy.

God, you are my joy. I praise you for loving and protecting me. I glorify your name for your goodness to all your people. Amen.

Praise the Lord in song, for He has done excellent things; let this be known throughout the earth.

Isaiah 12:5 NASB

WARMTH OF WELCOME

Do not neglect to show hospitality to strangers, for by doing that some have entertained angels without knowing it.

Hebrews 13:2 NRSV

The Bible tells us that the apostle Paul went to the riverbank outside the city of Philippi one day, where he spoke to a group of women who met there to pray. One, the merchant Lydia, enthusiastically embraced Paul's message, then opened her home to Paul and his traveling companions. We can learn from Lydia's example.

When you invite God into your life, his Spirit opens the door of your heart to others, showing you how to express hospitality through the warmth of your welcoming smile, the provisions of your busy kitchen, the gift of your undivided attention to each visitor.

Heavenly Father: Inspire in me the gift of hospitality so I may, both inside and outside my home, offer a welcome that is pleasing to you. Amen.

Remember Lydia, and consider all the ways you can open your home and your heart to others.

Be inventive in hospitality.

Romans 12:12
THE MESSAGE

LIBERATION

We have freedom now, because Christ made us free. So stand strong.

Galatians 5:1 NCV

The women's liberation movement of the 1970s brought about remarkable gains for women in education, employment, and legal rights. Few of us would willingly give up these hard-won advantages, but they cannot compare to the freedom God gives!

His magnificent liberty releases you from guilt, fear, and self-gratification, and allows you to experience complete harmony of body and soul. His freedom lets you move ahead in spiritual maturity and holy living, and by his authority you can count yourself as a worthy and purposeful child of God.

Celebrate your freedom today by exploring some of the most meaningful advantages of heart, mind, and soul that Jesus won for you.

Where the Spirit of the Lord is, there is freedom.

2 Corinthians 3:17 NCV

Dear God: Thank you for winning for me true freedom, freedom of the spirit. Release me from anything that threatens my priceless liberty in you. Amen.

WHAT THEY'RE SAYING

The integrity of the upright will guide them.
Proverbs 11:3 NKJV

*D*orcas was a member of the New Testament church. Known for her godly actions, consistent with her belief in Jesus, her life uplifted and encouraged believers and her character brought many others into the early Christian church.

Your godly reputation depends on character, the unwavering connection between what you believe and what you do, and between unseen matters of the spirit and observable conduct with family, friends, associates, and even strangers. Your words, choices, attitude, and lifestyle show God's will and purpose for your life, and people will recognize you as a woman of honor and goodness. Wherever you go, your reputation is a credit to you—and God.

Dear God: Guide my ways so my words and actions testify to your goodness and a godly reputation reflects your work in my life. Amen.

Keep your eyes focused on what is right, and look straight ahead to what is good.
Proverbs 4:25 NCV

FOR HIS GLORY

Be exalted, O God, above the highest heavens! May your glory shine over all the earth.

Psalm 57:5 NLT

There will be times when it is hard to contain the love you feel for God. Sunshine warms your face, a gentle breeze blows softly, and suddenly you are reminded of all the times you have experienced his blessings. They are more than you can number. He sustains you when trouble comes. He moves quickly to lift you up whenever you fall and cry out to him. He protects you as you drive along busy thoroughfares. When you wonder if he is listening to the prayers of your heart, he shows up in some miraculous way, letting you know that he hears every word.

He is God, and the earth is full of his glory. He also is the Lord, who loves you with an everlasting love. So trust him, because he is truly faithful.

I cry out to God Most High, to God who fulfills his purpose for me.

Psalm 57:2 ESV

I bow down before you, Lord. I am in awe of your greatness and in wonder of your infinite love. Thank you for your ceaseless grace. Amen.

March 30

GIFTED GROUP

There are different kinds of gifts, but the same Spirit. There are different kinds of service, but the same Lord.

1 Corinthians 12:4–5 NIV

God invites us to value the diverse skills and talents of others. This clearly implies the presence of at least one skill or one talent in each of us to be used for the good of all.

God's gifts to you may be obvious, and if so, he urges you to develop and broaden your talents so you can grow even more effective and productive in your given work. If you think God has left you off his gift list, think again. Consider what you do for the sake of other people, and name these things as your talents—then share them with all your heart.

Every desirable and beneficial gift comes out of heaven. The gifts are rivers of light cascading down from the Father of Light.

James 1:17 THE MESSAGE

Heavenly Father: Help me discover and embrace the unique gifts you have seen fit to give me, that I may use my talents in joyful service to others. Amen.

IT'S CATCHING

[God] will yet fill your mouth with laughter.
Job 8:21 NASB

Perhaps you have a friend whose effervescent laughter and joy lifts your heart. You can't help but share her joy of life.

A merry heart comes naturally as you grow closer to God and nurture your relationship with him. Refreshed by his words of hope, his promises, you become more open to the bright and playful aspects of life. You more fully appreciate the simple blessings surrounding you, and find heartfelt happiness in knowing all things rest in his hands. From there, your joy spreads to those around you.

Dear God: Grant me the ability to see and appreciate the humor in life and share the gift of a merry heart with those in need of laughter and joy. Amen.

Fill your heart with God's promises and let him show you the delightful side of his creation. His joy is contagious!

A merry heart makes a cheerful countenance.
Proverbs 15:13 NKJV

APRIL

*Incline your ear and hear the
words of the wise, and apply
your heart to my knowledge.*

PROVERBS 22:17 NKJV

OUT OF THANKFULNESS OR OBLIGATION?

How can I repay the Lord all the good He has done for me?

Psalm 116:12 HCSB

There will certainly be times when God requires you to obey him in something that you find extremely challenging or unpleasant, and you will be tempted to abandon what he has called you to. This is a test of your heart—of how you really view your relationship with God.

Are you serving him out of a thankful heart—willing to do whatever he tells you to? Or are you serving him out of obligation—with limits on what you will do on his behalf? Are you committed to him because of your overflowing love? Or are you trying to buy his affection through "good works"?

A difficult assignment can leave you wondering why you should continue trusting and serving him. But when you do, you become an authentic, living example of true praise and thanksgiving to God.

God, I want to serve you out of love and thanksgiving—not out of obligation. Help me to offer myself wholeheartedly no matter what you call me to do. Amen.

God, here I am, your servant, your faithful servant: set me free for your service! I'm ready to offer the thanksgiving sacrifice and pray in the name of God.

Psalm 116:16–17 THE MESSAGE

April 2

FOCUSED
CONTEMPLATION

*I think about you before I go to sleep, and my thoughts turn to
you during the night.*

Psalm 63:6 CEV

One of the most effective things you can do to better
your life is to go to bed praising God for his goodness. Doing this before you turn the light out lays the groundwork
for gratitude, thanksgiving, and praise at morning's first light.

Why is it important for you to remember God's faithfulness?

Because recalling his goodness motivates you to trust him for
the future. Remembering the times he has forgiven you teaches
you to be honest and admit your need for
him. Realizing that he is at work in your
life gives you hope for the day to come.

It is easy to forget all the wonderful
things God has done. But when you focus
on his goodness, it strengthens your spirit
and helps you to turn to him quickly no
matter what may arise.

> My whole being follows hard after You
> and clings closely to You; Your right hand
> upholds me.

Psalm 63:8 AMP

*Lord, help me focus
on your unfailing love
and praise you with
all my might. In your
goodness and grace I
will rest peacefully,
for you, Lord, are my
hope. Amen.*

April 3

FOREVER FRIENDS

[Jesus said,] "Greater love has no one than this, than to lay down one's life for his friends."

John 15:13 NKJV

riendship has been called a plant requiring constant care, and indeed, the delightful flowers of friendship bloom only with our commitment to faithfully nurture those relationships.

By willingly giving his life, Jesus forged a bond of eternal friendship between God and you, and his sacrifice provides an example for all his disciples to follow. He has shown you how to give of yourself to your friends by generously offering them your time and companionship, and willingly providing to each of them your unconditional love. Jesus has proven the fragrance of true friendship comes not in taking from but in giving to your friends.

Dear God: Renew in me a commitment to give of myself to my friends and do all within my power to nurture and strengthen my friendships. Amen.

The sweet smell of incense can make you feel good, but true friendship is better still.

Proverbs 27:9 CEV

WONDER WOMAN

Let the weak say, "I am strong."

Joel 3:10 NKJV

Perhaps you know about "Wonder Woman," the all-powerful comic book heroine of the same name, or maybe you remember the 1970s TV show based on her character. While the fictional fantasy entertains, God's power, strength, and wondrous acts are for real.

The spiritual strength you possess through God's Spirit gives you the ability to turn away from the crowd when it's going in the wrong direction. In life's troubles and times of hardship, God's stable, steady hand will see you through and bring about positive and productive ends.

In him, think of yourself as a woman with wondrous powers, and use your strength to achieve great things.

> O Lord, be gracious to us; we long for you. Be our strength every morning, our salvation in time of distress.
>
> Isaiah 33:2 NIV

Dear God: As I learn more about you, I stand in awe of your power. Grant me reliance on you, source of all true strength, when I face the trials and tests of life. Amen.

NOT NATURAL . . . SUPERNATURAL

There is no one who does good.

Psalm 14:1 NASB

Have you ever wondered if something within you fights against honoring God? If so, you are right. It is contrary to human nature to submit to him. People's natural inclinations can only lead to destruction; there is nothing inherently good about them.

When you begin to seek God, it is not by natural means; rather, he draws you *supernaturally* by his Spirit. In fact, when you believe in him to save you, he gives you his Holy Spirit to guide, teach, and transform you. It is then that you can obey him, that you can truly do good.

Through the power of God's Spirit, you can choose to honor him. Therefore, embrace the supernatural life and enjoy his extraordinary blessings. Because what he offers you is truly out of this world.

God, thank you for drawing me to you by your Spirit. Teach me the difference between your direction and my natural desires so I can always honor you. Amen.

From heaven the Lord looks down to see if anyone is wise enough to search for him.

Psalm 14:2 CEV

April 6

RESPONSIBLE ACTION

Let your light shine before men in such a way that they may see your good works, and glorify your Father who is in heaven.

Matthew 5:16 NASB

We know what it's like to begin an exercise program with high hopes, then find our energy flag as time passes. Without continued motivation, we're likely to quit and not reach our desired goal.

While God has provided your salvation, he warns you not to lose sight of it by becoming neglectful of your faith or taking it for granted. He reminds you to remain a responsible possessor of faith by exercising it in words and actions reflective of his presence in your life. In so doing, you win others to God by your conduct and you become a godly presence in a world in need of his peace and love.

Heavenly Father: In gratitude for the promise of eternal life, I want to live in a way worthy of the gift you have seen fit to give me. Amen.

It is God who works in you to will and to act according to his good purpose.

Philippians 2:13 NIV

THE MERCIFUL FATHER

God . . . does not retain His anger forever, because He delights in unchanging love.

Micah 7:18 NASB

*M*ercy is difficult to define, but we've all experienced it. Mercy saves and redeems and preserves all that it touches. It is like rain that falls on a parched desert and brings forth a multitude of new blossoms.

Although mercy is rare in the world around us, God is generous with his. He uses it to restore our "desert-dry" hearts and reawaken the dormant spirit. If you will receive his mercy, God longs to pour a full measure on you.

If you find that your spirit is in need of the restoration that God's mercy can bring, reach out to him. You will receive all that you need.

The Lord is compassionate and merciful.

James 5:11 NRSV

Dear God: I need your mercy to bring life back to the desert in my heart. Thank you for giving your mercy to me freely and generously. Amen.

April 8

SOMETHING TO OFFER

Those who fear You will be glad when they see me, because I have hoped in Your word.

Psalm 119:74 NKJV

When you hear the testimony of other believers, do you ever wonder, *God, why haven't I told others what you've done for me?*

Or do you think, *My story isn't as exciting as hers. I really have nothing to offer.*

Friend, this simply isn't true.

Jesus wants you to lift him up so he can draw people to himself, and one of the ways you exalt him is by telling others what he's done for you. The very anecdote that seems so insignificant to you could be exactly what someone else needs to hear to have faith in him.

Always remember that the hope you have in Jesus Christ is like a cool drink of living water to dry and thirsty souls. So offer all you have and trust him to satisfy them.

> I rejoice at Your word, as one who finds great spoil. . . . Those who love Your law have great peace, and nothing causes them to stumble.
>
> *Psalm 119:162, 165 NASB*

God, there are so many things you have done for me that need to be told. Teach me to tell others about you so they will have faith in you as well. Amen.

TRUTH TALKS

Love should always make us tell the truth. Then we will grow in every way and be more like Christ, the head of the body.

Ephesians 4:15–16 CEV

A friend excitedly relates her latest news, and you recognize it as something that could cause her future pain and sadness. Have you ever found yourself in this predicament? What do you say?

The Bible teaches us that real love always tells the truth. And you've probably already learned that offenses most often come not from what we say but from how we say it. Ask God to prepare your heart, wiping away any ulterior motives, pride, or judgmental attitudes. Ask him to make you his instrument of loving truth. Your courage could save a friend from a good deal of heartache.

Dear God: Grant me the courage and confidence I need to tell the truth in a world so much in need of your guidance, and help me always to speak in love. Amen.

The Lord . . . is pleased with people who tell the truth.

Proverbs 12:22 NIrv

GUIDANCE ON THE GO

Guide my steps by your word, so I will not be overcome by any evil.

Psalm 119:133 NLT

emale drivers are thought to be more willing than male drivers to ask directions when they're lost on the highway. Remember when you're feeling lost in life that God offers guidance to let us know we are on the right path.

Sometimes the unanticipated happens. You might see several available courses of action but aren't sure which one to choose. When you don't know which way to turn, never hesitate to ask God for directions. Let him point out the way he would have you go. Changes in your relationships, health, or situation can bring new challenges and opportunities. Asking God will help show you the way.

Dear God: So many times in my life I need your wisdom and guidance. Thank you for always being there for me. Amen.

The Lord will guide you continually, and satisfy your soul in drought. . . . You shall be like a watered garden.

Isaiah 58:11 NKJV

WHEN YOU MESS UP

You, O Lord, are good, and ready to forgive [our trespasses, sending them away, letting them go completely and forever]; and You are abundant in mercy and loving-kindness to all those who call upon You.

Psalm 86:5 AMP

The enemy's goal is to tempt you to yield to sin. He knows that even the smallest failure can cause guilt to rise up within you. If he can lead you to stumble spiritually or morally, he can further crush you with the lie that God wants nothing more to do with you. Yet nothing could be further from the truth.

The Lord hates sin because he loves you—because sin devastates your soul. However, when you confess your failings to him and turn away from them, God embraces you with deep affection and support.

Teach me, Lord God, to call out to you for help and strength rather than yield to temptation. And thank you for forgiving me when I mess up. Amen.

Never allow the enemy's accusations to keep you from experiencing God's forgiveness. The devil may want you to fall, but the Lord can lift your soul. He will never leave you, so call upon him and receive his pardon.

Every time I'm in trouble I call on you, confident that you'll answer.

Psalm 86:7 THE MESSAGE

WHAT IS WORSHIP?

Come, let us worship and bow down; let us kneel before the Lord our Maker. For He is our God, and we are the people of His pasture.

Psalm 95:6–7 NKJV

Some people talk about being in a great house of worship and sensing God's presence. The towering spires, stained-glass windows, and deeply carved wooden altar where private confessions are made are elements that can stir your heart with thoughts of his unconditional love, mercy, and grace.

Many times, however, the most sacred place is found in the quietness of your own room and in the stillness of your heart. This is where God personally meets with you, reveals himself to you through his Word, and teaches you how to live each day with hope and a sense of victory.

The Lord of heaven cannot be confined to a building or a single location. He is omnipresent—everywhere at all times. He is awesome in nature, and he is near to you right now.

Let us come before him with thanksgiving and extol him with music and song. For the Lord is the great God, the great King above all gods.

Psalm 95:2–3 NIV

God, I am in awe and wonder at your greatness. Thank your for extending your personal love to me and for the opportunity to live each day for you. Amen.

April 13

EYES WIDE OPEN

What happens when we live God's way? . . . We develop a willing-ness to stick with things. . . . We find ourselves involved in loyal commitments.

Galatians 5:22 THE MESSAGE

When you make a pledge to another person, you know every moment of every day will not be rosy. If it were, the pledge would not be meaningful. You count on experiencing times of joy and sadness, satisfaction and frustration, but your pledge takes precedence over all and keeps you going.

Your commitment to God requires the same understanding. You must accept what will happen—you will find delight, despair, and everything in between. For this reason, Jesus advises his disciples to count the cost before making a promise to follow him. Know, though, that you can count on him to be there for you every step of the way.

Dear God: Instill in me a willingness to give up anything that prevents me from giving myself wholeheartedly to your Spirit. I commit myself to you. Amen.

The eyes of the Lord range throughout the earth to strengthen those whose hearts are fully committed to him.

2 Chronicles 16:9 NIV

April 14

ENCOURAGING
OTHERS' SOULS

May those who fear You see me and be glad, because I wait for Your word.

Psalm 119:74 NASB

Today, you'll utilize talents that will benefit your work and life. Those have been given to you for your own survival and improvement.

Yet you also have spiritual gifts that are specifically entrusted to you for the sake of others. God imparted those gifts so you could be his instrument of blessing and encouragement to those in need. Whether you help, give, teach, pray, or serve, you represent God's comfort and provision to them.

Friend, understand that you've been given the wonderful privilege of showing

God, how would you have me encourage others today? Please empower me to bless those around me mightily with my spiritual gifts! Amen.

God's love to all the people who cross your path. So use your God-given gifts for his glory! Others will undoubtedly be encouraged and glad to have you around.

> Let your steadfast love comfort me according to your promise to your servant. Let your mercy come to me, that I may live; for your law is my delight.
>
> Psalm 119:76–77 ESV

AM I GOOD ENOUGH?

Lord, who can dwell in Your tent? Who can live on Your holy mountain?

Psalm 15:1 HCSB

salm 15 goes to the heart of humanity's deepest problem—is anyone worthy of living in heaven with God? You are told that you must be honest and kind and that you must keep all the Lord's commands and never do wrong to others. Reviewing these requirements, you may question whether you can ever truly meet God's standards.

That is as it should be. The inability to be *good enough* makes you aware of your need for God's help, which he graciously provided through the death and resurrection of his Son, Jesus Christ.

When you trust him for salvation, God covers you with his righteousness and makes you worthy of dwelling with God for eternity. So believe in him, trusting his provision. Because then you can rest in *his* goodness forever.

God, I know I cannot make myself worthy of heaven, so I trust you for salvation. Thank you for forgiving my sins and covering me with your goodness. Amen.

Such people will stand firm forever.

Psalm 15:5 NLT

WHO I AM

Love from the center of who you are; don't fake it.
Romans 12:9 THE MESSAGE

Many girls are taught to hide their true feelings behind a mask of pleasantries, and when they grow into womanhood, many continue their charade of benevolent words and acts. The mere surface appearance of goodness, however, is not enough.

God sees through our masks, and he reads what's really in our heart. Where he finds negative thoughts or cunning motives, he is able to bring about a change of heart so the mask can disappear, allowing genuine goodness to create affection, kindliness, and thoughtfulness to others.

Heavenly Father: Fill me with your Spirit so my love for others will be genuine and my words and actions an authentic reflection of who I am in you. Amen.

The harmony God works between private feelings and public behavior enables you to be forever free to show your true face to the world.

Love one another deeply, from the heart.
1 Peter 1:22 NIV

GOD'S MESSAGE

God takes particular pleasure in acts of worship—a different kind of "sacrifice"—that takes place in kitchen and workplace and on the streets.

Hebrews 13:16 THE MESSAGE

Ads on television and in fashion magazines reinforce a beguiling but false message: for true happiness, pamper yourself. God's message declares the opposite: for true happiness, deny yourself and pamper others.

God, who loved you before you were born and continues to love you and preserve your life today, never stops giving himself to you. When Jesus was born, he denied himself the glory and luxury of heaven to carry out his part of God's plan for salvation, and ultimately gave his life for the sake of yours.

God's Spirit in you prompts you to listen to his message: If you desire happiness for yourself, lavish it wholeheartedly on others.

Present your bodies as a living sacrifice, holy and acceptable to God, which is your spiritual worship.

Romans 12:1 NRSV

Dear God: Help me overcome the natural desire to indulge myself instead of serving the needs of others. Plant the desire to give unselfishly deep within my heart. Amen.

April 18

THE SEED OF
YOUR SORROW

*Those who plant in tears will harvest with shouts of joy. They
weep as they go to plant their seed, but they sing as they return
with the harvest.*

Psalm 126:5–6 NLT

This trouble you are facing has pierced your heart and
drawn your tears. You wonder why God would allow
it in your life—especially since your relationship with him has
been going so well. However, God wants to take you deeper—and
to do that he must dig into the tender soil of your soul.

Hebrews 12 explains, "It's the child he loves that he disciplines.
. . . At the time, discipline isn't much fun. . . . Later, of course, it
pays off handsomely, for it's the well-trained who find themselves
mature in their relationship with God" (vv. 6, 11 THE MESSAGE).

Friend, God is drawing you closer to
himself and growing the priceless beauty
of a godly character in you. His discipline
is difficult, but it is necessary to make you
the amazing woman he created you to be.

Then we were filled with laughter, and we
sang happy songs. . . . The Lord has done
great things for us, and we are very glad.

Psalm 126:2–3 NCV

*God, this situation is
really difficult, but I am
thankful that you have
a good purpose in it and
that you collect all of my
tears. Help me to trust
you even more. Amen.*

April 19

WISE WOMAN'S
WORDS

*The quiet words of the wise are more to be heeded than the shouting
of a ruler among fools.*

Ecclesiastes 9:17 NRSV

*D*o you remember the last time someone offered you meaningful words of advice, and the way the advice was given? In all likelihood, your friend spoke in a calm, thoughtful manner, and because she was gentle, you benefited from her knowledge and experience in a positive way.

When you believe your knowledge could help another person or your experience could save her from a mistake, share your insight in a kindly and affirming way. Sensitive subjects can be awkward and even embarrassing, but consider that your silence could cause the greater hurt.

Use your wisdom—your lessons learned, your failings overcome—to lift up others. It is the loving thing to do.

*God of All Wisdom:
Grant me wisdom to
know when to share
my thoughts with
others, and put in
my mouth words of
true helpfulness and
spiritual insight.
Amen.*

All wisdom comes from the Lord, and so do common sense and understanding.

Proverbs 2:6 CEV

NATURE DECLARES HIS PRAISE

Let the heavens be glad and the earth rejoice; let the sea and all that fills it resound. Let the fields and everything in them exult.

Psalm 96:11–12 HCSB

*I*t is easy to think, *When I see the Lord, I'll do this or say that.* The truth is that when you see him face-to-face, the only thing you will want to do is bow down and worship him. Words, if they are spoken, will only be those of praise and adoration. You will not be able to contain yourself or the love you feel for him. In fact, all of creation will exalt his holy name.

This is why it is so necessary to learn to praise him now. It is practice for what you will be doing for eternity. Honor him for his goodness, faithfulness, long-suffering, and provision for your every need. Sing songs of glory to his name today and every day—for surely he is worthy both now and forevermore.

God, there are times when I overlook all that you have done for me. Right now I want to thank you for taking care of all that concerns me. Amen.

The Lord is great! He should be highly praised. He should be feared more than all other gods because all the gods of the nations are idols. The Lord made the heavens.

Psalm 96:4–5 GOD'S WORD

TO YOUR HEALTH

*"I will restore health to you and heal you of your wounds," says
the Lord.*

Jeremiah 30:17 NKJV

In recent times great strides have been made in women's
medical care. Physicians are now aware more than ever
before of conditions and symptoms specific to women, and more
treatment options have become available.

God has never needed to increase his attention to you. He has
always been aware of, and provided, the care you need. Whenever
you are ill or in pain, he is there with his healing touch. Whether
your pain is of body, mind, or spirit, God will help you through
it. If you're hurting right now, reach out
to him for support. You are sure to feel
his comfort and his peace.

*Great Healer:
Bless the health-care
providers for all they
do each day. Thank
you for your healing
touch that surpasses
all earthly resources.
Amen.*

Beloved, I pray that all may go well with
you and that you may be in good health,
just as it is well with your soul.

3 John 2 NRSV

HIS HEALING ARROWS

Both the inward thought and the heart of man are deep. But God shall shoot at them with an arrow.

Psalm 64:6–7 NKJV

Have you ever gotten up in the morning and remembered some deed done to you as if it just happened? You try to shake off the memory, but you walk around all day feeling as though you're under a cloud of anger.

God does not want your bitterness to rob you of the power and joy he has for you. That is why he will target it like a bowman with an arrow, so that you will deal with the issue consuming your thoughts, energy, and emotions.

It is easy to cling to feelings of unforgiveness, anger, or resentment, but God calls you to do the opposite—to forgive and move beyond the hurt. When you let go of past sorrows, you are free to accept the blessings he has for you.

Lord, I am in awe of your awesome love. Thank you for revealing my old wounds and healing me of their pain. Truly you are wonderful! Amen.

Then all men will fear, and they will declare the work of God, and will consider what He has done.

Psalm 64:9 NASB

GOOD REASONS

I will hope continually, and will praise you yet more and more.

Psalm 71:14 NRSV

"I hope" reflects a wish, but when the Bible speaks of hope, the word refers to a conviction that God's promises are true.

When God's Spirit plants hope in your heart, you perceive your life in light of his purpose for you. You rely on his promise to protect you, guide you, forgive you, and bring you at last to live with him in heaven. Your conviction gives you cause for optimism even when things aren't going your way, because you have placed your hope in God's power and his pledge to work all things out for your good.

Take hold of hope and make it the light of your life.

Dear God: Strengthen my belief in your words and grant me sure and certain hope in your plan of salvation and promise of eternal life. Amen.

My soul claims the Lord as my inheritance; therefore I will hope in him.

Lamentations 3:24 TLB

April 24

POISED FOR ACTION

The Lord will be your confidence, and will keep your foot from being caught.

Proverbs 3:26 NKJV

*Y*ou can find any number of self-help books intended to bolster your confidence. In them, you may discover some useful ideas to improve your outlook, but the books rarely mention where genuine self-assurance comes from.

Teresa of Avila said, "Let us remember that within us there is a palace of immense magnificence." God says he lives within each believing heart, and he lives in you. The immense magnificence of God's Spirit in you is the reason you can be sure of yourself in any situation. This is the true source of self-confidence. Knowing that God lives within you, and will never fail you, means that no obstacle is too great.

> God has given us his Spirit. That is how we know that we are one with him, just as he is one with us.
>
> 1 John 4:13 CEV

Dear God: I'm in awe as I contemplate your presence within me. Your Spirit gives me all the assurance I need to handle every circumstance that comes my way. Amen.

GOING FORWARD

Encourage each other every day while it is "today."
Hebrews 3:13 NCV

omen who occupy the top echelons of corporations, who win awards for achievements in athletics or the arts, or who have achieved great things in society often attribute their success to someone who urged them to persevere until they reached their goal.

As you continue to build your relationship with God, surround yourself with faith-encouragers. These fellow travelers will bolster your spirit and inspire you with their wisdom and experience. In the same way, others will certainly need your expertise and insight to urge them ahead as they mature in the faith.

Dear God: I thank you for the encouragement I receive from those around me. Help me to be an encouragement to others. Amen.

God would have you generously give and gladly receive encouragement as you persevere in your walk of faith.

We pray that our Lord Jesus Christ and God our Father will encourage you and help you always to do and say the right thing.

2 Thessalonians 2:16–17 CEV

IN THE PROPER PERSPECTIVE

By [the help of] God I will praise His word; on God I lean, rely, and confidently put my trust; I will not fear. What can man, who is flesh, do to me?

Psalm 56:4 AMP

Sometimes the negative words of others can be devastating. Because of them, you struggle with thoughts of doubt, fear, or condemnation. However, the psalmist learned how to put the words of others in the proper perspective, and you can too.

When you believe in Jesus Christ as your Savior, you gain a fresh sense of unshakable hope and peace. The connection you have with him empowers you to stand firm against the most deceptive thought or attack. You discover how to say as the psalmist did, "I will not fear!" because you know that your Lord defends you no matter what others may say.

Therefore, open your heart and mind to Jesus' personal love and care for you. You will not be disappointed by what you find.

> You know how troubled I am; you have kept a record of my tears. . . . You have rescued me from death and kept me from defeat. And so I walk in the presence of God, in the light that shines on the living.

Psalm 56:8, 13 GNT

God, thank you for providing the hope I need to get through every situation. I will find hope and peace in your word. Amen.

ALLOW FOR CHANGE

To everything there is a season, a time for every purpose under heaven.

Ecclesiastes 3:1 NKJV

Women experience change intimately, changing from girlhood to maturity and from fertility to menopause. Rarely do we welcome change with open arms. God, who put in place the seasons of nature and the stages of a woman's life, offers another perspective.

Changes in your life, whether initiated by you or by other factors, invite you to discover God in deeper and rewarding ways. Changes shake up your status quo and send you seeking a new level of comfort. When your searching leads you closer to God, your times of change build your courage and strength.

Resist the urge to run. Embrace change instead as a way to know God better.

[God] changes times and seasons.

Daniel 2:21 NIV

Dear God: When I go through times of change, help me to choose a positive, productive response and grant me contentment with each new phase in my life. Amen.

April 28

YES!

Let us be self-controlled, putting on faith and love as a breast-plate, and the hope of salvation as a helmet.

1 Thessalonians 5:8 NIV

ome women claim the freedom to act as they choose. They seem to be having the time of their lives. You ask yourself why God tells you no in regard to certain behavior.

God's rules assist you in making life-affirming choices. He knows the world offers many attractive options, but not all of them are positive. While you can see the negative consequences of some, you cannot see far enough ahead to know the outcome of others. God sees, even to eternity, and he guides you toward those paths that will render a happy and prosperous future.

Rest assured, his no is your yes to a full, free, and joyful life.

> Prepare your minds for action; be self-controlled; set your hope fully on the grace to be given you when Jesus Christ is revealed.
>
> 1 Peter 1:13 NIV

Dear God: Thank you for guiding me in the right paths, and keep me faithful when I face a choice between self-gratification and self-control. Amen.

April 29

PRAISE FROM ALL
THAT EXISTS

*All creation, come praise the name of the Lord. Praise his name
alone. The glory of God is greater than heaven and earth.*

Psalm 148:13 CEV

All of nature praises God, and yet sometimes it may
seem unnatural to you. Why?

The creation reflects the glory of the Creator. A flower does not
form its lovely petals of its own accord. The stars do not raise themselves up into the sky or shine on their own. The sea does not fill itself.

Perhaps you are far too dependent upon yourself for beauty,
success, and fulfillment. You don't naturally praise God because
you've forgotten your purpose for existing—reflecting his glory
and growing in his love.

*God, I do praise you!
Show me how to reflect
your glory and express
your love so I can
exalt you even better.
Certainly you are
worthy of my deepest
adoration. Amen.*

Living in dependence and praise to
God is the very best, most wonderful life
you could ever imagine. So open your
heart to the One who created you, and
discover all the beauty, success, and fulfillment he's planned for you.

Let every created thing give praise to the
Lord, for he issued his command, and they
came into being. He set them in place forever and ever.

Psalm 148:5–6 NLT

April 30

SET ME FREE

I run in the path of your commands, for you have set my heart free. Teach me, O Lord, to follow your decrees; then I will keep them to the end.

Psalm 119:32–33 NIV

Have you ever yearned to be free from your responsibilities? It isn't unusual for you to feel this way—especially if the tasks you've been doing haven't been initiated by God. When you fail to follow God's course for your life, the activities that were once enjoyable may become burdensome obligations.

However, Jesus said, "Take my yoke upon you and learn from me, for I am gentle and humble in heart, and you will find rest for your souls. For my yoke is easy and my burden is light" (Matthew 11:29–30 NIV). The work he gives you to do sets you free because he takes the responsibility for its success upon himself.

God, help me to keep in step with your plan by doing what you have given me to do. Strengthen me to do your will, my God, so I don't become weary. Amen.

Are you wearied from burdens and obligations? Then trade your yoke for his and do as he says. Surely you'll find freedom for your soul.

I have gained perfect freedom by following your teachings.

Psalm 119:45 CEV

MAY

*How amazing are the deeds of
the Lord! All who delight in him
should ponder them. Everything he
does reveals his glory and majesty.
His righteousness never fails.*

PSALM 111:2—3 NLT

137

May 1

PEACE, IF . . .

I am listening to what the Lord God is saying; he promises peace to us, his own people, if we do not go back to our foolish ways.

Psalm 85:8 GNT

A deep sense of peace is yours when you turn your thoughts to God. There is always hope when you choose to listen to him instead of to the negative messages of the world. God's Word reminds you that when you draw near to him, you will find the comfort you need. When you are still in his presence, he provides the wisdom and insight to meet every challenge victoriously.

Thank you, dear God, for the times you express your unconditional love toward me. Teach me your ways so I can always abide in your peace. Amen.

King David knew that with God's aid he could advance against a mighty army and subdue his enemies. Because of his faith, the Lord strengthened him and gave him many astounding triumphs.

Not every day brings an emergency or a call for action, but many do bring a need to remember how greatly God loves you. So seek him, and receive his peace.

God will soon save those who respect him, and his glory will be seen in our land. Love and truth belong to God's people; goodness and peace will be theirs.

Psalm 85:9–10 NCV

May 2

GOOD CHOICES

I do not run without a goal. I fight like a boxer who is hitting something—not just the air.

1 Corinthians 9:26 NCV

Throughout history, dedicated women have worked to establish educational and social opportunities for girls and women. Their perseverance has opened a world of opportunity.

With opportunity comes the privilege and obligation to make wholesome, meaningful, and God-pleasing choices. You will know you have done so when you know the satisfaction of working toward an objective bigger than yourself and using your gifts unselfishly on those around you. Your ideals keep you moving toward that objective, persevering even when it's not personally convenient, keeping you focused on truth and goodness.

Dear God: Thank you for the opportunities available to me. Guide me as I choose my life's goals and plans. Amen.

With God, your aim is lofty and you reach high because you have looked on high for your goals and ambitions.

Run in such a way as to get the prize.

1 Corinthians 9:24 NIV

THE OASIS

Our lives get in step with God and all others by letting him set the pace.

Romans 3:27 THE MESSAGE

If you're like most women, your calendar overflows with things to do and places to go. Slowing down is very difficult in this fast-paced world.

Like a cool oasis, God offers a haven from the pressure of activity and the physical and spiritual fatigue it can bring. He wants you to live life to the fullest, so he opens his arms and welcomes your weary spirit. He says "slow down" not to hold you back but to refresh and restore you, leaving you confident in his love.

Dear God: Thank you for giving me this time of peace and contemplation. I need and desire my time of rest in you. Amen.

The most important thing on your busy calendar each day is the time you spend in his embrace. With that, all things are possible.

Oh, that my steps might be steady, keeping to the course you set.

Psalm 119:5 THE MESSAGE

BLESSED WITH REST

It's useless to rise early and go to bed late, and work your worried fingers to the bone. Don't you know he enjoys giving rest to those he loves?

Psalm 127:2 THE MESSAGE

You know all there is to accomplish and how little time there is to finish it all; so you try to press on—straining your body and mind to continue. However, it is useless. You cannot go any further. The weariness has completely overtaken you.

What can you do?

First, you must accept that you need rest. Second, you must acknowledge that you're having so much trouble because you're trying to do everything in your own strength rather than God's strength.

The task may be too big for you, but it's not too big for him. So express your faith in him by resting in his care. Give your burden to him, and trust him to renew you with his energy, wisdom, and efficiency. You will be amazed at all he will accomplish through you.

God, it is challenging to give this burden to you, but I will trust you with it. I rest with confidence knowing that with your help so much more will be accomplished. Amen.

Unless the Lord builds a house, the work of the builders is wasted. Unless the Lord protects a city, guarding it with sentries will do no good.

Psalm 127:1 NLT

THE PRIVILEGE OF HIS PRESENCE

How happy is the one You choose and bring near to live in Your courts! We will be satisfied with the goodness of Your house, the holiness of Your temple.

Psalm 65:4 HCSB

God will challenge you to do many wonderful things in this life—he will encourage you to launch out in faith with the tasks he calls you to do. But there is something that brings an even greater degree of satisfaction than anything you can experience on a human level, and that is time spent in quiet devotion to him.

Though your life may seem too full to take time to be alone with him, consider this: He is never too busy to be with you. His one consuming desire is for you to know him. When you begin to do this, even the smallest of activities will take on new meaning.

God, for far too long, I have dismissed your efforts to touch my heart. Please open my life up to you so I may experience all you have for me. Amen.

So spend time with him today and enjoy the awesome privilege of being in his presence. Surely it will be the best time you have all day!

You answer us in amazing ways, God our Savior. People everywhere on the earth and beyond the sea trust you.

Psalm 65:5–6 NCV

THE GOOD LIFE

Good people can look forward to a bright future.

Proverbs 13:9 NCV

What makes for a good life? Laughter and happy times come to mind. You might also be thinking of those times you did the right thing without worrying about what the future would bring.

In those positive moments, God steps in with words of comfort and assurance. He praises us for following his commandments and gives us the strength to keep on going. Then he adds a promise. He tells us to look forward to tomorrow with hope and expectation. He says we can get excited about the future.

Rest in the peace of knowing you're doing the right thing. And smile, because the best is yet to come.

I know the thoughts that I think toward you, says the Lord, thoughts of peace and not of evil, to give you a future and a hope.

Jeremiah 29:11 NKJV

God in heaven: When things look hopeless to me, help me look to you for my hope. In you alone I put my trust. Amen.

GOOD BOUNDARIES

*Lord, you have assigned me my portion and my cup; you have made
my lot secure. The boundary lines have fallen for me in pleasant places.*

Psalm 16:5–6 NIV

God created you at this appointed time in history and in your
unique circumstances for a reason. Your experiences have
not only shaped your personality and values, but they will affect how
you serve God and to whom you are able to minister.

Although your life may be difficult at present, it is not a mistake
that you are where you are. God has set the boundaries of your
life not for harm, but for good. Not to cause you pain, but to give
you purpose.

*God, I praise you for
working all things out
for my good. Thank
you for using my
life's boundaries for
your glory, the benefit
of others, and my
edification. Amen.*

You may not understand how God
could use your situation, but he will bless
you abundantly if you will allow him to
lead you. Therefore, listen to him and seek
his wisdom in your circumstances. Then
rejoice as he turns your limitations into
wonderful opportunities.

I will praise the Lord who counsels me—
even at night my conscience instructs me. I
keep the Lord in mind always. Because He
is at my right hand, I will not be shaken.

Psalm 16:7–8 HCSB

A New Beginning

God, make a fresh start in me, shape a Genesis week from the chaos of my life.

Psalm 51:10 THE MESSAGE

hoices and decisions of all kinds confront us on our life's journey, and sometimes we make mistakes. It has nothing to do with being a woman, and everything to do with being human. That's why God does something about our human mistakes. He forgives them. He not only gives us a clean heart but also a fresh start.

Perhaps you feel guilty for something you have said or done. No matter how serious it may have been, God waits for you with open arms. He stands ready to dry your tears, forgive you, and comfort you. Let him give you a new beginning.

I will give you a new heart and put a new spirit within you.

Ezekiel 36:26 NKJV

Dear Father: Help me find peace in your forgiveness. Show me the way to a new beginning in my life. Amen.

HELP WITH HEAVY LIFTING

Share each other's troubles and problems, and so obey our Lord's command.

Galatians 6:2 TLB

Most of us would ask for help lifting a one-hundred-pound trunk, but we avoid getting help with heavy burdens of heart and spirit. God never intended that we bear problems and troubles by ourselves. That's why he places us among others—friends and family—so not one of us needs to stumble under a full load.

Think of the women you know and consider the many unique skills and abilities they represent. Don't forget to include your own. Count up their backgrounds, experiences, and gifts, and you will realize you're among heavy lifters who can assist one another with heart-heavy burdens of all kinds.

Together you can move mountains.

[Jesus said:] "Come to Me, all who are weary and heavy-laden, and I will give you rest.

Matthew 11:28 NASB

Heavenly Father: By your Spirit, make me a willing sharer of others' burdens, and give me the grace to ask my friends for help with my troubles and problems. Amen.

May 10

THE REAL THING

[Jesus said,] "No one is good but One, that is, God."

Matthew 19:17 NKJV

As children we were admonished to be good, to mind our manners, play by the rules, and see to the needs of others. But at some point in every woman's life, she realizes that as hard as she tries, she can only do so much. She will never be able to be good in the eyes of everyone.

Dear God: You know that I have always tried to be good. As I get to know you, place your pure goodness in my heart. Amen.

Each woman must come to understand that pure goodness comes from God. It is woven inextricably into his very nature, the essence of who he really is. When you enter into relationship with him, he shares his unblemished nature with you and urges you to keep your eyes on him rather than on the expectations of others.

O taste and see that the Lord is good.

Psalm 34:8 NRSV

LET GO

Give your burdens to the Lord, and he will take care of you. He will not permit the godly to slip and fall.

Psalm 55:22 NLT

here are some issues so personal that you feel you cannot give them up—not even to God. The thought of entrusting your beloved burden to his care is more than you can handle. It is as if you would be allowing a piece of your heart to be torn from you.

Friend, let go. You have made this situation an idol, and you are clinging to it as if it could make you happy. Yet all that it has brought you is heartache.

God, it is so difficult for me to relinquish control in this area. Nevertheless, I also know it will destroy me if I do not. Please help me overcome my fears and teach me to trust. Amen.

Your battle is not with God, it is with yourself. Moreover, if you release this burden to him, he will take care of it better than you ever could. He will also heal you of all the pain it has caused you.

So let go. And let God show you how sufficient he truly is.

He will redeem my soul in peace from the battle which is against me.

Psalm 55:18 NASB

ALWAYS WITH YOU

I feel completely secure, because you protect me from the power of death. I have served you faithfully, and you will not abandon me.

Psalm 16:9–10 GNT

oneliness can strike for many reasons: loss, rejection, and separation from loved ones. Yet if you allow it to consume you, alienation, insecurity, and thoughts of unworthiness can become your private prison, one that is incredibly destructive and difficult to escape from.

Friend, God wants to free you from your loneliness through his enduring presence and healing care. With him, you never have to fear being alone, because he assures you of his unfailing love. As you grow closer to him, he not only teaches you to have a fulfilling relationship with himself, but with others as well.

God, I thank you for never leaving or forsaking me. Thank you for freeing me from the bondage of loneliness and teaching me to love others as you do. Amen.

So whenever the bondage of loneliness begins to close around your heart, trust the One who will never leave you or forsake you. You will be glad you did.

You will show me the path that leads to life; your presence fills me with joy and brings me pleasure forever.

Psalm 16:11 GNT

May 13

SONG OF THANKS

Overflowing grace God has given to you. Thank God for this gift too wonderful for words!

2 Corinthians 9:14–15 NLT

When the prophetess Miriam led the Israelites in song, she proclaimed how God had worked to deliver his people from oppression. To this day, gratitude to God stems from an awareness of the great things he has done and continues to do.

Heavenly Father: Thank you for all you have done and continue to do in my life. Let me respond with a heart of gratitude and with words of thanks and praise. Amen.

Through the ministry of Jesus, God delivered you from the oppression of earthly desires and the chains of cynicism, guilt, and unbelief. He made available the assurance of his mercy and compassion, and he opened to you the knowledge of his willingness to call you his own and lead you on a path of holiness. This is his utmost desire.

In thanksgiving, let your life proclaim his wonderful work!

O give thanks to the Lord, for He is good.

1 Chronicles 16:34 NASB

THE SHELTER OF HIS PROMISES

Even in my suffering I was comforted because your promise gave me life.

Psalm 119:50 GNT

When the sun is shining, it's hard to imagine the approach of a violent storm. However, a change in environment can take place quickly. What begins as a beautiful morning may become a dark and threatening day.

However, you don't have to allow a sudden shift in climate to cause you to feel discouraged or defeated. God has vowed never to leave your side, and he is always at work on your behalf. He knows your struggles, and has promised to provide the wisdom, strength, and courage you need to stand firm in your faith.

God, whenever pressures build and the storms of life assail, help me to recall your wonderful promises so that I will not be tempted to give up. Amen.

Therefore, hide his promises and principles within your heart, so you'll have the hope you need for times of tempest. Because then, no matter how strong the winds of adversity blow, the Word of God will guide you to safety.

Remember your promise to me, your servant; it has given me hope.

Psalm 119:49 GNT

UNPREDICTABLE

Clouds and darkness are round about Him [as at Sinai]; righteousness and justice are the foundation of His throne.

Psalm 97:2 AMP

God is never surprised by the unpredictable events of this world. He is never shaken, and he is never changed by anything that happens. He is the same today, tomorrow, and forever, and he is in control of all things.

Lord, I praise you because nothing is beyond your control. Today if I have an unexpected challenge, please remind me of your constant and unyielding love. Amen.

Why can you face the future with a clear sense of hope and promise? Because he takes care of all that concerns you. Whether the stock market rises or falls, God remains the same. Though health issues come and go, he will always prove to be faithful.

You have a sure hope for your life that holds steady no matter how stormy or bright life becomes—and that is the hope you have in Jesus Christ.

The mountains melt like wax at the presence of the Lord, at the presence of the Lord of the whole earth. The heavens declare His righteousness, and all the peoples see His glory.

Psalm 97:5–6 NKJV

A LIGHTER LOAD

[God] comforts us every time we have trouble, so when others have trouble, we can comfort them with the same comfort God gives us.

2 Corinthians 1:4 NCV

Declaring "I don't want to get involved" or "I don't know what to say," some women avoid a troubled acquaintance or pass by a sorrowing friend. We've all done that at one time or another.

The next time someone needs comfort and you don't know how to help, stop and pray. Ask God to comfort that person just as he has comforted you in times of sadness and sorrow. Ask his Holy Spirit to make his love and compassion real to her. Then ask what you can do to help. You can be confident that God knows best, and he will show you what to do to be a blessing.

"Comfort, comfort my people," says your God.

Isaiah 40:1 NLT

God of Comfort: Just as I find my solace in you, empower me through your Spirit to ease the sorrows of others by bringing to them the comfort of your love. Amen.

*He has granted to us his precious
and very great promises, so that
through them you may become
partakers of the divine nature.*

2 PETER 1:4 ESV

REALLY CLEAN

Happy are those who live pure lives, who follow the Lord's teachings.

Psalm 119:1 NCV

As a teenager, you probably thought about the concept of purity of life in terms of saving sexual relations until marriage. While the idea of purity of life certainly includes sexual morality, it encompasses far more than a single aspect of a woman's life.

God's idea of purity directs your thoughts to subjects of worth and value that give birth to words and actions consistent with God's commandments. The kind of purity God has in mind for you isn't afraid to confront the world's loose morals with boldness, because its foundation is in the power of God's eternal truth.

Genuine purity begins in the heart that is washed clean by God's Spirit.

> *Dear God: Grant me the resolve to see where I need to embrace purity in my life, and instill in me the willingness to allow your Spirit to cleanse me. Amen.*

Oh, worship the Lord in the beauty of holiness!

1 Chronicles 16:29 NKJV

HE WILL NEVER FAIL YOU

Let us hold unswervingly to the hope we profess, for he who promised is faithful.

Hebrews 10:23 NIV

ll people fail at one time or another. The best-laid plans can come up short. God will never fail you. He is the one constant in your life that you can trust, utterly and without reservation.

You won't have to wonder if he'll be there tomorrow or whether he will still love you. He will. You can count on that and on all the other promises God has made to you in the Bible—more than 5,000 in all. Though he may not do things the way you expect, you can be certain that he will never, ever let you down. He is faithful.

Dear Father: I place my heart in your hands and I trust in your faithfulness. Thank you for always being there for me. Amen.

The Lord is faithful in all his words, and gracious in all his deeds.

Psalm 145:13 NRSV

THE WORD THAT ENDURES

What you have done will be praised from one generation to the next;
they will proclaim your mighty acts.

Psalm 145:4 GNT

People do different things to have a lasting influence on others' lives. Many volunteer, some provide meals for families in crisis, and others offer advice. All these things are good, but do they count for eternity? Do they have a lasting effect?

There is something you can do that God promises will endure—and that is telling others about him and directing them to the Bible. "The rain and snow come down from the heavens and . . . water the earth. They cause the grain to grow, producing seed for the farmer and bread for the hungry. It is the same with my word. I send it out, and it always produces fruit. It will accomplish all I want it to, and it will prosper everywhere I send it" (Isaiah 55:10–11 NLT).

Everyone will know the mighty things you do and the glory and majesty of your kingdom. Your kingdom will go on and on, and you will rule forever. The Lord will keep all his promises.

Psalm 145:12–13 NCV

God, I want to have an eternal influence on this world for your name's sake. Please teach me the Bible so I can instruct others and lead them to you. Amen.

HE HAS NOT FOREGOTTEN

He has remembered his steadfast love and faithfulness to the house of Israel. All the ends of the earth have seen the salvation of our God.

Psalm 98:3 ESV

here will be times when you wonder if God has forgotten his promises to you. He never does. Months or years may pass, but regardless of the length of time, always remember the plans he has for you.

God does not operate according to anyone's schedule. Joseph spent years in Egyptian exile before he realized what the Lord wanted to do in his life. The time he spent in prison was not wasted. God was preparing him for an even greater purpose and only time would reveal what this was. His responsibility was to wait obediently for the Lord to work.

This same principle applies to you. The next time you are tempted to become anxious or impatient, remember God always blesses those who are committed to waiting for and trusting him.

God, I want to honor you with my life. Please forgive me for pushing forward when you want me to wait, and help me to know when you want me to advance. Amen.

The Lord has made His victory known; He has revealed His righteousness in the sight of the nations.

Psalm 98:2 HCSB

May 21

FACING FEARS

Do not fear, for I am with you, do not be afraid, for I am your God; I will strengthen you, I will help you, I will uphold you with my victorious right hand.

Isaiah 41:10 NRSV

When you were a little girl, you may have been afraid to enter a darkened room or sleep without a night-light. In our youthful imaginations, all sorts of dangers lurked in the dark.

Heavenly Father: Thanks to you, I have everything I need to face the future with boldness and strength. Amen.

As adults, we know light dispels dark shadows and the best way to deal with uncertainties is to shine a light into dark places. Faith in God is the lantern that banishes shadows and lights the way to true happiness. Your faith in God's unwavering presence gives you courage. If the dangers are real, you can face them, with his help.

Walk with God, because he walks with you. You can rest at ease in his light.

Fear not, O land; be glad and rejoice, for the Lord has done marvelous things!

Joel 2:21 NKJV

SWEET VINDICATION

Show Your marvelous lovingkindness by Your right hand, O You who save those who trust in You from those who rise up against them.

Psalm 17:7 NKJV

Whenever you serve God, there will be those who do not understand your devotion to him and may even oppose what he has commanded you to do. Their heated words and antagonism may be discouraging, but be strong. Continue to do what is right—honoring the Lord.

As hard as they try, no one can prevent God from fulfilling his purpose for you. In addition, when you honor him faithfully, his loving character will shine through you in a manner that they will not be able to deny.

Therefore, instead of growing angry with your adversaries, pray that they will accept the freedom that God offers. Then, whether or not they decide to follow him, you will have succeeded in doing what is right and keeping your heart clean. That is all the vindication you really need.

God, I do pray for those who oppose your work in the world. Help them to accept the truth of your love and help me to always honor you. Amen.

You have tested my heart; You have examined me at night. You have tried me and found nothing evil.

Psalm 17:3 HCSB

DRAWING FROM THE WELL

God is the real source of wisdom and strength.

Job 12:13 CEV

What if you could go each morning and draw wisdom and strength from a pure and bottomless well? No matter how depleted you might feel as you close your eyes at night, you would know that you soon would be refreshed and replenished. There actually is a well just like that.

God invites you to come to him each day, to draw from his never-ending supply of wisdom and strength. His resources are endless, and he's promised never to deny you when you ask for his help. He's always there waiting, ready to give you what you need to take on another day with grace and confidence.

Oh, what a wonderful God we have! How great are his riches and wisdom and knowledge!

Romans 11:33 NLT

Heavenly Father:
I need a fresh drink of
your wisdom each day.
Thank you for inviting
me to come and be
refreshed. Amen.

MUTUAL FEELINGS

All of you be of one mind, having compassion for one another.

1 Peter 3:8 NKJV

ompassion is a wonderful thing. By an act of your will, you enter into another person's pain, sorrow, or sadness. You help shoulder the load. That's what God did when he had compassion toward you. He came down to where you were. He took your pain and sorrow and suffering on himself. That's what true compassion is all about.

Two things happen when you show compassion for others: You find yourself feeling good because God created you to find fulfillment helping others—and you find it every time you extend a hand to someone in need. You also open yourself up to receive the compassion others extend when you need it.

Dear God: Increase my willingness to act with compassion toward others, and open my heart to receive with joy and gratitude the care and comfort others lavish on me. Amen.

Are your hearts tender and compassionate? Then make me truly happy by agreeing wholeheartedly with each other, loving one another, and working together with one mind and purpose.

Philippians 2:1–2 NLT

ENOUGH FOR TODAY

Blessed are those whose strength is in you. . . . They go from strength to strength, till each appears before God.

Psalm 84:5, 7 NIV

God has given his Word to you for several reasons. When you study it, you not only gain insight into his ways and principles, you also receive direction and encouragement. The psalms are an excellent source of hope and comfort, especially when you are battling some intense trial.

David faced many challenges in his lifetime, but he always found the strength he needed to overcome every threat by recalling God's goodness and promises to him.

Lord, you know all things. Please help me to understand your Word and your will for me. Encourage me according to my deepest need. Amen.

Have you learned to do the same? When trouble comes, do you turn to the Bible and ask the Lord to speak to you, or do you rush to call a friend?

The support of loved ones is essential, but the amazing love of an omnipotent God can never be replaced.

How lovely is your dwelling place, O Lord Almighty! My soul yearns, even faints, for the courts of the Lord; my heart and my flesh cry out for the living God.

Psalm 84:1–2 NIV

THE REWARDS
OF OBEDIENCE

A man who obeys the Lord will surely be blessed.

Psalm 128:4 GNT

Why not just do what you want—forgetting God's commands and following your own desires? You know the answer, because there have been times that you've done that very thing. You've gone against God's instruction and have caused your own grief. Your plans left you unsatisfied, lonely, and full of regret.

Just the opposite has been true whenever you've submitted yourself to him. The tasks may have been difficult, but his presence energized you and you were filled with his indescribable joy. You saw his amazing work in your life and experienced the blessings of being in his will.

You know how rewarding obedience can be—so do as he says in every situation! Because "God is fair; he will not forget the work you did and the love you showed for him" (Hebrews 6:10 NCV).

Happy are those who respect the Lord and obey him. You will enjoy what you work for, and you will be blessed with good things.

Psalm 128:1–2 NCV

God, thank you for taking note of and blessing everything I do in obedience to you. Thank you for always leading me in the best way possible. I submit myself to you. Amen.

THE MIGHTY JUDGE

The Lord is still in his holy temple; he still rules from heaven. He closely watches everything that happens here on earth.

Psalm 11:4 TLB

It's easy to feel powerless in this world, especially if you're a woman. But when you place your trust in God, you can stand strong and confident, knowing you have a friend and advocate in the highest of places. It is someone who is looking out for your interests, someone who is perfectly just and steadfastly good.

You need not accept quietly everything that life lays at your feet. Lift up your eyes to heaven. Plead your case before the mighty judge of all. He loves you, and because of that, you can be sure he will hear you and do what is best for you.

*Loving Father:
I bring my cause
before you today. I
place it in your hands,
and I thank you for
providing a place of
rest for me. Amen.*

True wisdom and real power belong to God; from him we learn how to live.

Isaiah 30:18 THE MESSAGE

IMPOSSIBILITIES

*Take a good look at God's wonders—they'll take your breath
away. He converted sea to dry land; travelers crossed the river
on foot. Now isn't that cause for a song?*

Psalm 66:5–6 THE MESSAGE

The night the storm broke out on the Sea of Galilee, the waves began to swell, and a hard rain beat down. Fear consumed the disciples' minds and hearts. How could they possibly survive the tempest?

Yet their anxiety was unfounded, because Jesus was with them. When their cries woke him, Jesus stood up and did the impossible—he commanded the wind and the waves to be still, and both obeyed (Mark 4:35–41).

The same is true for you whenever you experience the overwhelming storms of life. Though they arise unexpectedly, there is no reason to fear, because the Lord is with you. When you place your trust in him, he will provide the protection you need to get through every trial—even the kind that seems impossible.

> Bless our God, you peoples! And make the voice of His praise to be heard, who keeps our soul among the living, and does not allow our feet to be moved. For You, O God, have tested us; You have refined us as silver is refined.

Psalm 66:8–10 NKJV

*Words cannot express
my love for you, Lord.
You are my refuge,
and I am overwhelmed
by your greatness and
humbled by your love
for me. Amen.*

BEEN THERE, DONE THAT

There are many rooms in my Father's house. . . . I am going there to prepare a place for you.

John 14:2 NCV

When the subject turns to motherhood, women who are mothers speak up, while those without children remain silent. On the subject of heaven, however, non-experienced people have no qualms about speaking out on the topic!

> *Dear Jesus: Thank you for the promise of heaven. Keep me listening to you, the only one qualified to tell me about the peace and joy awaiting me there. Amen.*

During his earthly ministry, Jesus could speak about heaven with full authority because he had been there and he knew he was going to return there. He spoke with experience, having seen the glories of heaven, the angels, and all God's beloved people gathered around. He described what it looks like and what you can expect when you get to your heavenly home.

When the subject comes to heaven, listen to the expert—Jesus.

He puts a little of heaven in our hearts so that we'll never settle for less.

2 Corinthians 5:5 THE MESSAGE

WATCHING WHAT YOU DO

The naive believes everything, but the sensible man considers his steps.

Proverbs 14:15 NASB

Certain encounters will not take you anyplace good, whether it's someone in a back alley offering to sell you a brand-new television for thirty-five dollars or an e-mail from a widow in Africa looking for a person to help her gain access to her late husband's twelve-million-dollar bank account.

Traps are everywhere, but a wise person looks where his foot is going to land before he takes a step. Without becoming cynical, you can learn to read people, understand their body language, and discern false motives from true. Ultimately, the

God, save me from being gullible. Keep me from being conned. Let me be wise without becoming needlessly suspicious. Amen.

only person who can never be conned is God himself. That's why you rely on him and the counselors he has placed around you to keep you safe.

> Where there is no counsel, the people fall; but in the multitude of counselors there is safety.
>
> Proverbs 11:14 NKJV

PERFECT IN EVERY WAY

The Lord is righteous in all His ways, gracious in all His works.

Psalm 145:17 NKJV

In the world we live in, it is said that absolute power corrupts absolutely. This is not so with God. His ways are always right—wise, just, and free of any wrong. Know that he will always do what's best for you. He will never fail you, and he will never abandon you. He will only bring goodness to your life.

As you open your heart to him, his nature will change your life. You will begin to see things differently and more clearly. Wrong thoughts will be swept away by good thoughts. Your actions will follow as you come to know God, and become more and more like him.

I am the Lord; I act with steadfast love, justice, and righteousness in the earth, for in these things I delight, says the Lord.

Jeremiah 9:24 NRSV

*Merciful Father:
I desire that my thoughts and actions be right, just as you are. Thank you for seeing me as I should be rather than as I am. Amen.*

JUNE

I keep the Lord in mind always.
Because He is at my right hand,
I will not be shaken.

PSALM 16:8 HCSB

A FAITHFUL SOUNDING BOARD

*Give ear to my prayer, O God. . . . Give heed to me and answer me;
I am restless in my complaint and am surely distracted.*

Psalm 55:1–2 NASB

The troubles come from every side, leaving you almost paralyzed due to their intensity. You try to concentrate—to get something done. However, the problems you face bombard your thoughts until you cannot separate one from another.

You are weary, but cannot sleep. You want to escape, but feel so bound by the situation that you cannot take your mind off it. You think no one could possibly understand the toll it is taking on your soul.

However, there is One who does.

Friend, no matter what troubles you are facing, there is no reason for despair. God hears you and will help you. Call to him—lay your burdens at his feet. He never tires of hearing you and is always available to speak peace to your soul.

God, thank you for understanding the terrible stress I am experiencing and for listening to my prayers. And thank you, dear Lord, for helping me as only you can. Amen.

I call to God; God will help me. At dusk, dawn, and noon I sigh deep sighs—he hears, he rescues.

Psalm 55:16–17 THE MESSAGE

June 2

STANDING STRONG

Let us hold fast the confession of our hope without wavering, for He who promised is faithful.

Hebrews 10:23 NKJV

If you pay close attention to what's happening around you, it's easy to lose perspective. Horrors like AIDS, famine, wars, brutal dictators, oppression, and the evil that preys on the poor and powerless seem to be closing in on every side.

But one truth eclipses all the pain, suffering, and injustice. God brings light and hope to a dark, hopeless world. He is faithful and true in a world filled with selfishness and deceit. He is the one person you can count on; he is the one person who will never let you down.

God, I will not relinquish my hope to the evil in this world. I will trust in you. When I grow faith—and I will—strengthen me. Amen.

The next time you feel like the world is closing in, look up. Keep your eyes fixed on God. That's where your hope and strength will come from.

> We are hard-pressed on every side, yet not crushed; we are perplexed, but not in despair; persecuted, but not forsaken; struck down, but not destroyed.
>
> 2 Corinthians 4:8–9 NKJV

DAUGHTER OF GOD

Do everything without complaining or arguing, so that you may become blameless and pure, children of God without fault.

Philippians 2:14–15 NIV

f you're a mother, you've heard it—"Do I *have* to?" As a child, you probably said it yourself. A child's rebellion is nothing to boast about, and resentful obedience brings no pleasure.

God wants more than begrudging compliance to his wishes. From his children of all ages, he welcomes willing obedience when he speaks, including those times when the reason he makes a certain request remains unclear, or when the particular sacrifice he asks of you seems difficult and burdensome.

Heavenly Father: Grant me a heart of willing submission to your will and a sincere desire to please you as your obedient daughter. Amen.

When you eagerly listen to God's voice and gladly carry out his requests, you're a child of God giving your heavenly Father something to be pleased about.

Just look at it—we're called children of God! That's who we really are.

1 John 3:1 THE MESSAGE

GETTING OVER YOURSELF

Not for our sake, God, no, not for our sake, but for your name's sake, show your glory. Do it on account of your merciful love, do it on account of your faithful ways.

Psalm 115:1 THE MESSAGE

*Y*ou may be tempted to believe your life is no more than a mundane, ordinary routine. You may do your daily tasks the same way every day, and mediocrity may characterize your tiresome existence. However, you don't have to stay in a rut.

God is creative. He wants you to grow beyond the boundaries you have set for yourself and experience the abundant life he created you for.

When you see limitations, he sees gateways to new opportunities. How does he help you expand your horizons—especially when life seems to be one predictable step after another? He challenges you to view life from his perspective.

Trust him to use you to encourage others and to expand your narrow limits, because there are many exciting opportunities for you to enjoy when you place your faith in him.

God, help me to accept new challenges so I can grow in my faith in you. Open doors so that I can become all that you want me to be. Amen.

Our God is in heaven doing whatever he wants to do. . . . May you be blessed by God, by God, who made heaven and earth.

Psalm 115:3, 15 THE MESSAGE

June 5

GIFT OF THE HEART

Be kind and good to others; then you will live safely here in the land and prosper.

Psalm 37:3 TLB

Women often devote much of their lives to the happiness and well-being of others. To some, it is simply a gift of the heart from being blessed by God with a giving nature.

God speaks to you about the way he would have you respond to others, no matter what role or roles you play. It is his desire that all people work together in a spirit of love, compassion, and generosity. Mutual respect, shared affection, and reciprocal kindness lead to godly relationships. In some relationships, God invites you to take the first step. In each relationship, your giving nature is the key to doing God's will here on earth.

Dear God: Thank you for all the relationships in my life. Grant me the generosity of spirit to bless each relationship with godly love. Amen.

Whoever has the gift of encouraging others should encourage.

Romans 12:8 NCV

June 6

WHEN YOU PRAY

My cry to him reached his ears. Then the earth reeled and rocked; the foundations also of the mountains trembled and quaked.

Psalm 18:6–7 ESV

avid was thankful. As he recalled the many times God had delivered him from dangerous foes, he could not help but testify about the Lord's unfailing faithfulness. Whatever the situation, no matter how dire the trial, God *always* answered his prayers.

However, you may wonder what happens when *you* pray. Does God respond to you as he did David? Yes, he does. He moves heaven and earth to answer anyone who calls to him with faith and sincerity. Although his reply may not be what you expect, he never fails to do what is in your best interest and what will ultimately fulfill his purpose for you.

> *God, thank you for hearing my prayers and for answering me as you did King David. Truly, you are faithful, loving, and worthy of all my praise. Amen.*

Therefore, call out to the Lord with whatever concerns you. David found him exceedingly faithful, and there is no doubt you will too.

He brought me out to a wide-open place; He rescued me because He delighted in me.

Psalm 18:19 HCSB

June 7

ENCOURAGED AND HOPEFUL

Hope does not disappoint, because the love of God has been poured out within our hearts through the Holy Spirit.

Romans 5:5 NASB

True hope is hard won. It begins with the daily pressures you face. Through them, you grapple with the truth of God—who he is and what he has promised.

Pressures produce perseverance—the ability to keep going and be patient because you see that God has never let you down. And that perseverance produces character, because your life is not based on daily changes but on God's eternal truth.

That truth produces hope, which does not disappoint because you have seen his goodness and you know you will see it again.

Through it all you know him and love him more—and that is truly a reason to feel encouraged and hopeful.

God, today I praise you for pouring out your love and giving me hope. Even in the daily pressures, you are doing wonderful things. Amen.

Let us rejoice and exult in our hope of experiencing and enjoying the glory of God.

Romans 5:2 AMP

CREATED FOR YOUR PLEASURE

God spoke: "Let us make human beings in our image, make them reflecting our nature so they can be responsible for the fish in the sea, the birds in the air, the cattle, and, yes, Earth itself."

Genesis 1:26 THE MESSAGE

Environmentalism has emerged as a topic for debate among political leaders, activists, and conservationists, but God had something to say about environmentalism at the time he spoke the world into existence. He gave humankind the privilege of being the crown of his creation as well as the responsibility of caring for his creation.

Let your gratitude for the world God fashioned for your pleasure and well-being prompt you to take a lively interest in issues surrounding clean air, soil, and water—gifts both to you and to generations to come. And show your respect for him by dealing kindly with all the living creatures of land, sea, and sky.

Creator-God: You have created a place of beauty and a resource for food and water. Enable me to do my part in protecting what you have made. Amen.

The Lord is the eternal God, Creator of the earth.

Isaiah 40:28 CEV

WHEN OTHERS DISAPPOINT

Do not trust influential people, mortals who cannot help you. When they breathe their last breath . . . their plans come to an end.

Psalm 146:3–4 GOD'S WORD

Don't get caught in the trap of thinking others will fulfill you or give you the joy you long for. Whether you're hoping for someone to love, help, or honor you for some achievement, it's possible that they will let you down. That disillusionment could crush your spirit.

God, I acknowledge that I put too much emphasis on the help and opinion of others. Please help me to trust you and look only to you for help and approval. Amen.

Your first reaction may be to blame God. Understand, however, that he was not the one who disappointed you. In fact, if you had kept your eyes on him instead of that person, your heart would not be broken. Rather, you would be growing deeper in your relationship with him.

When others fail you, use it as an opportunity to refocus on God, who will always lead you in the best way possible.

The Lord sets prisoners free and heals blind eyes. He gives a helping hand to everyone who falls. . . . The Lord God of Zion will rule forever! Shout praises to the Lord!

Psalm 146:7–10 CEV

June 10

INSIDE OUT

Be content with what you have.
Hebrews 13:5 NRSV

*P*erhaps you know a woman who simply radiates inner peace. In all likelihood, her contentment has nothing to do with how much money she has or her station in life. These external things cannot bring true satisfaction. Soul-deep peace comes from the inside.

No matter what circumstances surround you in life right now, you can possess the priceless treasure called contentment. It starts with knowing yourself as a woman loved by God, and it blossoms as you fully accept his will for your life. Joyously embrace those blessings he gives and continues to give, and you will find that inner peace you want and deserve.

God of peace: I give myself and all I am to you. Grant me the serenity of a heart and mind at peace in you. Amen.

The fear of the Lord leads to life: then one rests content, untouched by trouble.

Proverbs 19:23 NIV

June 11

YOUR TRUSTWORTHY GOD

May they know that You alone—whose name is Yahweh—are the Most High over all the earth.

Psalm 83:18 HCSB

There will be times when you cannot speak or defend yourself. Perhaps you are even given a chance to tell your side of the story, but it is as if the Holy Spirit has sealed your lips. He often does this so you will be still and allow him to speak for you.

God, thank you for answering my prayers. Even when I wait for you to defend me, I know that you will be faithful to reveal the whole truth. Amen.

Friend, if another person is bent on accusing you of something you did not do, give God the opportunity to reveal the truth. You bear his name, and when you act in obedience to him, you can be sure he will defend you in a manner better than any you could possibly imagine.

The Lord works in amazing ways and can change the course of any human plan. Be patient and trust him, because his vindication is coming.

O God, do not keep silent; be not quiet, O God, be not still.

Psalm 83:1 NIV

PAIN FROM THE PAST

They have afflicted me from my youth; yet they have not prevailed against me.

Psalm 129:2 NKJV

Of the words you will never forget, how many of them are negative? The hurtful things people say and do may stay with you a long time. Even if you've forgiven them, they affect the way you view yourself—especially if they occurred during your formative years.

God wants you to understand that he sees you as his dearly beloved daughter. He can transform your opinion of yourself through the truth of the Bible and through his tender love and heal the pain that others have caused in the past.

God, thank you for setting me free from the hurtful things others have said. Transform my understanding, and make my life an example of your marvelous grace. Amen.

Don't continue to give those who hurt you power over your life. You're a child of God—a recipient of his everlasting love and salvation. Act like it. Trust him to give you the freedom from the past you yearn for.

The Lord always does right, and he has set me free from the ropes of those cruel people.

Psalm 129:4 CEV

THE IMPORTANCE OF HOLINESS

Exalt the Lord our God, and worship at His holy hill; for the Lord our God is holy.

Psalm 99:9 NKJV

*P*eople often think that doing a certain activity will make them holy. There is only one way to begin the journey into holiness, and that is through a personal relationship with Jesus Christ.

Even though the Lord spent three years with the disciples, they still had problems that they had to overcome. Peter was impetuous; Thomas was doubtful; and the others worried whether Jesus would do what he had promised.

However, when the Holy Spirit came and he renewed their minds, they began to respond to problems and difficulties the way Jesus had. They drew even nearer to him and sought to be holy—just as he is holy.

The same is true for you. The closer you grow to Christ, the more you will be inspired to live a pure life that honors him.

Lord, remove everything within my life that would prevent me from becoming like you. I love you and want my life to honor you in every way. Amen.

Mighty King, lover of justice, you have established fairness. You have acted with justice and righteousness.

Psalm 99:4 NLT

June 14

A WISE WOMAN

Wisdom is a tree of life to those who embrace her; happy are those who hold her tightly.

Proverbs 3:18 NLT

We equate wisdom with remarkable perception and insight earned through experience. We often attribute wisdom to grandmothers who have overcome a lifetime of hardships with grace and courage. God, however, opens wisdom to all, regardless of age and situation in life.

When you study and meditate on God's Word, you gain understanding and you begin to learn more and more about the relationship he desires to have with you. You start to look beyond what your physical eyes can see and what your human reason can comprehend. You begin to grasp things of the Spirit made understandable only through the Spirit.

Today, let God make you a wise woman.

Women who have lived wisely and well will shine brilliantly, like the cloudless, star-strewn night skies.

Daniel 12:3 THE MESSAGE

Heavenly Father: Teach me those things known only by you so that I may gain knowledge of the spirit and wisdom of the heart. I desire to become wise in your ways. Amen.

HE IS WAITING

*You, the Lord God, are kind and merciful. You don't easily get angry,
and your love can always be trusted.*

Psalm 86:15 CEV

*S*omeone is waiting for you—it's God! And he's determined to wait as long as it takes. As long as you have breath, he will be there, hoping that you will turn your face to him, and return his love for you. He is patient and forgiving.

He doesn't care if you've ignored him in the past or even rejected him. Like a father longing for the return of his wayward child, he never gives up hope. And should you turn to him, he will not throw the past at you. He will simply say, "Welcome home, my beautiful child. I have been waiting."

The Lord is slow to anger, and abounding in steadfast love.

Numbers 14:18 NRSV

*Dear God: Thank you
for patiently waiting
for me, for never giving
up, for receiving me
without reservation.
Amen.*

HIS CHERISHED NAME

I will give thanks to your name, O Lord, for it is good. For he has delivered me from every trouble.

Psalm 54:6–7 ESV

William Shakespeare wrote, "What's in a name? that which we call a rose by any other name would smell as sweet." Yet when considering God's name, it carries with it meaning that should not only give you comfort, but confidence as well.

Take heart that when you read the Bible and see "Lord" in all capitals, it is an indication that it is a transliteration of *Yahweh*, which means, "I Am." In God's name is his character—the declaration that he is the ever-present Lord, who will never fail you.

He is faithful, wise, all-powerful, loving, and able to help you no matter what happens—just as he has been throughout history and will always be forevermore.

> *My God, the great I Am, thank you for being faithful and trustworthy in my life and in the lives of all your people. May your name be cherished forever. Amen.*

What is in his name? Everything—for in his wonderful name is the assurance that the One you love is truly worthy of all your adoration.

God, save me by Your name, and vindicate me by Your might!

Psalm 54:1 HCSB

WOMAN OF PRAYER

Whatever you ask for in prayer with faith, you will receive.
Matthew 21:22 NRSV

We know communication builds healthy relationships, and most of us go to great lengths to maintain open interaction between ourselves and our loved ones.

Prayer provides you the privilege of communicating with God and building on your relationship with him. He invites you to pray regularly and often, offering him your cares and concerns, your needs, hopes, and desires. Even though he already knows everything you're telling him, he also knows you need to articulate your thoughts to him, your loving friend and generous provider.

Communication being a two-way street, he speaks to you through Scripture. The more you listen, the more you know how to pray.

Dear God: I pray that our lines of communication will always be open. Thank you for hearing me. I truly desire to become a woman of prayer. Amen.

When you call on me, when you come and pray to me, I'll listen. When you come looking for me, you'll find me.
Jeremiah 29:12–13 THE MESSAGE

YOUR HEART, HIS HOME

This is my resting place forever. Here is where I want to stay. I will bless her with plenty.

Psalm 132:14–15 NCV

When you accept Jesus as your Savior, he marks you as his own. Ephesians 4:30 (GNT) explains, "The Spirit is God's mark of ownership on you, a guarantee that the Day will come when God will set you free." In other words, God's own Holy Spirit dwells within you—connecting you to him forever.

You cannot lose your relationship with God because it's not based on anything you can do or should refrain from. However, when you sin, you will recognize the dishonor of it because his Spirit is in your heart, saying, "Stop resisting me, beloved! Trust me. Rest in me. I will satisfy you and give you plenty."

God, thank you that I don't need to fear losing you when I sin. Help me to live a life of holiness and hope so that your home in my heart can stay beautiful forever. Amen.

Your heart is his home, and he works to keep you spotless, pure, and beautiful. So don't fear losing him. Rather, acknowledge when your heart needs to be cleansed.

O Lord, arise, and come to your resting place.
Psalm 132:8 GOD'S WORD

June 19

TO ALL PEOPLE

God blesses us so people all over the earth will fear him.

Psalm 67:7 NCV

Whether you realize it or not, showing up at church on Sunday is not the only way to express your love for God. Your life is a living testimony to others. Through your words and actions, you reflect your core beliefs, desires, faith, and fears.

My greatest desire, God, is for others to see you in and through my life. Help me to share your love with everyone I meet. Amen.

When you care for another person freely rather than out of obligation, you are expressing God's love. When you tell someone about the reason for the hope you have, you honor God.

Do you view those around you as he views them—with love, respect, and compassion? Do you share your blessings with them so that they will know the Savior? God knows your heart and how you choose to live each day. Therefore, honor him with everything you say and do so that others may know him and be saved.

Our God, be kind and bless us! Be pleased and smile. Then everyone on earth will learn to follow you, and all nations will see your power to save us.

Psalm 67:1–2 CEV

FACTS OF LIFE ETERNAL

By his Spirit [God] has stamped us with his eternal pledge—
a sure beginning of what he is destined to complete.

2 Corinthians 1:21–22 THE MESSAGE

ou have picked up this book and are reading these words. Do you know what that says about you? It says loudly and clearly that God's Spirit is at work in you!

God's Spirit at work in you proves two things: First, God has claimed you as his own and you belong to him. Second, God's claim means he has plans for you. He plans to stay close beside you today and every day of your life, and he plans for you to live with him forever in heaven.

You're a woman who belongs to God today, tomorrow, and forever.

Heavenly Father:
Because I am yours,
I can live today with
confidence and look
forward to living with
you in heaven forever.
Amen.

Having believed, you were marked in him with a seal, the promised Holy Spirit.

Ephesians 1:13 NIV

THE BUILDER
OF GREATNESS

Your gentleness has made me great.

Psalm 18:35 NKJV

God uses each challenge you experience to mold you into a person of significance and excellence. This does not imply he is making you wealthy or famous by the world's standards; rather, it means he is preparing you to reveal his glory.

Perhaps this seems unlikely to you. Maybe you once thought yourself special, but the years have destroyed the dreams that once thrilled your heart. Yet just as God took the shepherd David and made him a king, he can lift you out of your ordinary situation and reveal your wonderful potential, if you will let him.

Will you accept the trials that come as his training and allow him to build greatness in you? It is your choice. So embrace the future that is better than you can imagine.

God, thank you for seeing more in me than I see in myself. I trust you to use every situation to develop your godly excellence in me. To you be all the glory. Amen.

Lord, You light my lamp; my God illuminates my darkness. With You I can attack a barrier, and with my God I can leap over a wall.

Psalm 18:28–29 HCSB

UNPARALLELED GREATNESS

Shout aloud and sing for joy, people of Zion, for great is the Holy One of Israel among you.

Isaiah 12:6 NIV

You have a powerful friend. He is more powerful than any world leader. There's no chance that he will ever be voted out of office or forced off his throne. His reign is eternal; his greatness unparalleled. He has placed a million suns in the reaches of space and fixed the planets in their magnificent orbits. This great and wonderful God cares about you.

You may never fully understand the extent of your good fortune, but it is yours just the same, along with all the benefits that come with knowing such a mighty God. Rejoice. All things are possible for you.

Dear God: I am in awe of your power and majesty and humbled that someone like you would want me. I reach for your extended hand. Amen.

Yours, O Lord, is the greatness, the power, the glory, the victory, and the majesty. Everything in the heavens and on earth is yours, O Lord, and this is your kingdom.

1 Chronicles 29:11 NLT

June 23

LIFTED VOICE

Speak up for those who cannot speak for themselves, for the rights of all who are destitute.

Proverbs 31:8 NIV

In a New Testament story Jesus encounters a funeral procession. A widow had lost her only son. Jesus touched the boy and restored his life. He not only brought back the son to his grieving mother but also restored her dignity and her livelihood, for without a male family member to provide for her, she faced a life of destitution.

Today, young children, special-needs adults, and the elderly rely on others to care for and about them. God appeals to people to willingly and faithfully see to the well-being of others. He calls you to speak out for those who lack the voice or clout to be heard, and to see to their needs.

Heavenly Father: Grant me the courage to lift up my voice on behalf of those who lack strength, power, or resources to make their needs and wants known. Amen.

Blessed is the person who is kind to those in need.

Proverbs 14:21 NIrV

June 24

FILLED WITH WISDOM

If any of you lacks wisdom, he should ask God, who gives generously to all without finding fault, and it will be given to him.

James 1:5 NIV

No matter how knowledgeable a woman may appear, not one of us can claim competence in all circumstances. Sooner or later we're faced with a problem, a situation, or a stage in life in which we have to admit we're helpless.

When you're at a loss for answers, God welcomes your admission of need, because your realization of your human inadequacy allows God to fill you with his wisdom. He wants to lavish on you his understanding so you can discern his will and his solutions, and most of all, enjoy his transcendent peace.

Offer your limitations to him and receive his boundless wisdom in return.

Dear God: When I'm most at a loss to know what to do, place in me a heart open to your wisdom, the source of all knowledge and truth. Amen.

There's nothing better than being wise, knowing how to interpret the meaning of life.

Ecclesiastes 8:1 THE MESSAGE

WORTH REPEATING

God looked down from heaven on all people to see if anyone was wise,
if anyone was looking to God for help.

Psalm 53:2 NCV

Whenever you read something more than once in Scripture, it is because it is important. This is the case with Psalm 53, which is strikingly similar to Psalm 14.

Its message is certainly worthy of repetition—God peers down from his throne in heaven, watching for people who are looking for him. He wants to answer the searching heart and show his love to any who call upon him.

God, I want to love you with all my heart, soul, mind, and strength. Thank you for making yourself known to me and for teaching me your wonderful ways. Amen.

Are you seeking God? Do you long to experience his presence in a deep, meaningful way? Then realize that this desire within you is one he answers with a resounding "Yes!" He is gazing at you, friend, and he is delighted that you want to know him. Surely he will reveal himself to you in a powerful way.

How happy the people of Israel will be when God makes them prosperous again!

Psalm 53:6 GNT

HEART OF COMPASSION

Honor God by accepting each other, as Christ has accepted you.

Romans 15:7 CEV

From early school days, you may remember the one little girl no one seemed to like, and even today you may be able to name a woman spurned by others for obvious reasons, or for no discernible reason at all.

God asks of you a heart of compassion for the person others shun, for this is the kind of person Jesus made a point to speak to and to whom he extended his merciful, healing touch. With a welcoming smile, a kind word, and thoughtful gestures, you bring God's love to the people he cares about, those perhaps not readily accepted by others, but like you, precious in his sight.

Be imitators of God as dear children. And walk in love, as Christ also has loved us.

Ephesians 5:1–2 NKJV

Dear God: Grant me a compassionate heart and enable me to reach out to those whom others shun, so all may know of your deep love for every soul on earth. Amen.

WHAT EVERY WOMAN WANTS

I will be with them in trouble. I will rescue and honor them.

Psalm 91:15 NLT

God has placed within you a deep desire to be honored and respected. Every woman feels it. The great Aretha Franklin even sang about it—R-E-S-P-E-C-T. But so often we think we have to demand it. Those who try, soon find themselves frustrated and disappointed.

Dear God: Thank you for honoring me with your love. Teach me to honor you with my life. Amen.

True honor comes from God. It's his gift contained in his great love. As you respond, it becomes his reward for living in accordance with his will. It's his way of saying you have pleased him, blessed him, and made him proud.

Forget about seeking honor from others. The honor that comes from God will satisfy you to the depths of your soul.

Worthy are You, our Lord and our God, to receive glory and honor and power.

Revelation 4:11 NASB

June 28

THE EARTH'S
TRUE MASTER

Tremble, O earth, at the presence of the Lord.
Psalm 114:7 ESV

The earth is full of the glory of God—his absolute majesty inhabits every corner. Nothing you face today can or will change this truth—no heartache, no sorrow, and no disappointment. This may be a fallen world—one that has been tainted by sin—but soon God will return in power and might. He will restore all that has been broken.

God, forgive me for becoming so concerned about my problems and fearful of earthly threats. Your love is awesome; teach me to worship only You. Amen.

Every created thing is subject to his command because he is the Maker and King of all that exists. So regardless of how disjointed life seems, remember he is greater than all you fear. You can rest in his presence and find all the goodness, love, mercy, gentleness, kindness, and blessing you need. The fact that the sovereign God of the universe watches over you should fill your heart with joy, hope, and peace.

God brought his people out of Egypt. . . . When the sea looked at God, it ran away, and the Jordan River flowed upstream.

Psalm 114:1, 3 CEV

June 29

A SONG TO SING TOGETHER

Shout praises to the Lord, everyone on this earth. Be joyful and sing as you come in to worship the Lord!

Psalm 100:1–2 CEV

*N*othing in this world can bind individuals together like a vibrant faith in Jesus. In fact, the normal things that divide people tend to melt away when they allow the abundant love of Christ to flow through them.

Believers were always meant to be unified. In fact, Revelation 7:9–10 (GNT) says that one day people from "every race, tribe, nation, and language" will together call out, "Salvation comes from our God, who sits on the throne, and from the Lamb!"

So next time you feel lonely or as if you don't belong, reach out to another Christian and ask what Jesus is doing in their life. Soon enough, you will find your heart knit together with them in songs of praise to the Lord.

God, thank you that I have a song to sing with every other believer — a song of praise to you! Truly, you are worthy of all honor and glory! Amen.

Realize that the Lord alone is God. He made us, and we are his. We are his people. . . . Enter his gates with a song of thanksgiving. Come into his courtyards with a song of praise. Give thanks to him; praise his name.

Psalm 100:3–4 GOD'S WORD

GODLY BUSINESS

A faithful employee is as refreshing as a cool day in the hot summertime.

Proverbs 25:13 TLB

*Y*ou might deal with bosses, clients, customers, staff members, and assistants every day. Even if your work is in your home, you will invariably encounter others as you carry out your daily routine. God challenges you to take the lead in building and maintaining God-pleasing work relationships.

Choose to respect others, seeing them as women and men God loves, and treat them with kindness and compassion. Remember them in your prayers, taking their needs to God and asking him how you can serve and support them as they go about their duties and responsibilities. Bring God's Spirit into every business relationship; show genuine care for those God has placed in your life.

> *Heavenly Father: Help me become an instrument of your love and compassion for others as I go about the business of my day. Above and beyond those I report to at work, let me remember that I report to you. Amen.*

Let the loveliness of our Lord, our God, rest on us, confirming the work that we do.

Psalm 90:17 THE MESSAGE

JULY

I will sing of the tender mercies
of the Lord's unfailing love forever!
Young and old will hear of your
faithfulness. Your unfailing love
will last forever.

PSALM 89:1–2 NLT

GIVE GOD
THE GLORY

Pride ends in a fall, while humility brings honor.

Proverbs 29:23 TLB

From our youth we are taught not to be arrogant. Sometimes, however, we remember the lesson all too well and we cannot think of ourselves as gifted, valuable, and worthy women. Godly modesty is grounded in the satisfaction of knowing everything you are comes from him. Consider the progress you have made already in your spiritual journey. Recognize the work of God's Spirit in you and contemplate his wondrous ways. Where did all this come from?

Open yourself to the overwhelming joy of being his chosen instrument, and take great pleasure in the woman you are. Then, give God all the credit and praise for what you have become.

Dear God: Grant me a heart of true modesty and eyes to recognize your continuing work in my life. To you I give the glory! Amen.

The humble will inherit the land, and will delight themselves in abundant prosperity.

Psalm 37:11 NASB

IN NEED OF DELIVERANCE?

Out of the depths I have cried to You, O Lord. . . . There is forgiveness with You, that You may be feared.

Psalm 130:1, 4 NASB

Are you your own worst enemy? Are you holding yourself back through your destructive behavior and negative outlook?

The truth is, you cannot escape yourself, and there are issues that you cannot solve on your own. You have wounds you do not know how to heal, sins you cannot forgive yourself for, and walls built up in your heart that you are unable to overcome by yourself.

God can deliver you from all those things. You will only remain your own worst enemy if you refuse to allow him to work in your life.

Do not make that mistake! Rather, cry out to him. Admit your weaknesses. Trust him to rescue you. Rely on his wisdom, strength, and love.

God *can* and *will* help you. However, you must first be willing to be saved. Are you?

> I wait eagerly for the Lord's help, and in his word I trust.
>
> Psalm 130:5 GNT

God, I admit that I often sabotage myself in so many ways. Please help me. I need you and want to trust you. Please, God, heal what I cannot. Amen.

HIS VERY BEST

"Oh that My people would listen to Me. . . . I would feed you with the finest of the wheat, and with honey from the rock I would satisfy you."

Psalm 81:13, 16 NASB

Many people spend a great deal of time and money trying to find a way to feel safe, secure, happy, and peaceful. However, nothing you do apart from Jesus Christ has the ability to satisfy all of your needs and desires.

Large sums of money can vanish. People can walk away. Positions of power and fame can end in disgrace. Nothing this world has to offer can ensure future success or security. The one thing you can bank on is this: When God tells you he will satisfy you with the finest of wheat, he will give you his very best.

God withholds nothing from you. All that you need you will have, and you will never lack for anything.

I took the world off your shoulders, freed you from a life of hard labor. You called to me in your pain; I got you out of a bad place. I answered you from where the thunder hides.

Psalm 81:6–7 THE MESSAGE

At times it is hard to imagine how you will meet all my needs, but, Lord, you always do — and your provision is always perfect! Amen.

HIS TO LOVE

The God who is in his holy dwelling place is the father of the fatherless and the defender of widows. God places lonely people in families.

Psalm 68:5–6 GOD'S WORD

Have you truly opened your heart to the wondrous love that God has for you? You may say, "Oh, I know he loves me," but do you realize that his love for you is so great that he thinks about you constantly? He longs to give you good things, and when your heart is turned toward him in devotion, he is blessed.

You do not have to wait until you "feel" the love of God—his love is a reality that is always present with you. No sin can prevent him from loving you, and nothing is greater or has more power than his love. Rather, he gives his wonderful love to you

Draw me ever nearer to you, Lord, so that I will know the fullness of your love. In you I hope, and I give myself to you wholeheartedly. Amen.

freely, unconditionally; and the closer you grow in your relationship with him, the more you learn how faithful, strong, and true his care for you really is.

Thanks be to the Lord, who daily carries our burdens for us. God is our salvation.

Psalm 68:19 GOD'S WORD

WHEN THINGS SEEM UNFAIR, REMEMBER

I will thank You and confide in You forever, because You have done it [delivered me and kept me safe]. I will wait on, hope in and expect in Your name, for it is good.

Psalm 52:9 AMP

Before David ever took the throne of Israel, he had many heartbreaking experiences. At one point, he ran from King Saul and asked for help from the priests of Nob. Although the priests did not know Saul was pursuing David, the king put them to death for aiding his enemy.

You can imagine how David felt when he heard what had transpired—in fact, Psalm 52 records his thoughts. It was so unfair—the priests were merely trying to help him. Why would God allow it?

Yet remember, even when life does not seem fair, God is still in control.

Are you experiencing circumstances that seem completely counter to what God promised you? Do not despair. Hope in the Lord, because he will work everything out for your good in time.

God, thank you for helping me. When things seem unfair, I will trust you—remaining confident that you will transform this situation for my good and your glory. Amen.

I am like a flourishing olive tree in the house of God; I trust in God's faithful love forever and ever.

Psalm 52:8 HCSB

A STORY TO TELL

The heavens declare the glory of God, and the sky above proclaims his handiwork.

Psalm 19:1 ESV

All the wonders of the heavens declare the glory of God and proclaim his exquisite handiwork. And guess what? You do too.

When you believe in God, you become a living psalm, a walking demonstration that he exists, he is faithful, and he does all things well. People will experience his presence through the words you speak, your attitude, and even your actions toward them. They will realize that the God of grace loves them and wants to illuminate their life with his joy, mercy, and salvation.

Is that what you are saying with your life? Are you shining brightly as a light to those who need God's hope? You have a story to tell, so do it well. It may make an eternal difference to those who hear you.

Let the words of my mouth and the meditation of my heart be acceptable in Your sight, O Lord, my strength and my Redeemer.

Psalm 19:14 NKJV

God, I am so inspired to tell others your story. Guide my words and my heart so that I can honor you and encourage others to know you as well. Amen.

FAITH-FULL FINANCES

He who gathers money little by little makes it grow.

Proverbs 13:11 NIV

During Jesus' earthly ministry, a number of women regularly provided provisions for him and his disciples. Those women serve as an example to us of how to use financial resources in an unselfish and God-honoring way.

Dear God: Teach me to use my God-given financial resources in a responsible manner that honors you and to see to the needs of others before my own. Amen.

Your faith directs all aspects of your life, and God provides guidelines on how he would have you handle your monetary assets. Consider how your financial decisions will benefit and bring goodness into the lives of others, and ask God for his wisdom and discernment.

Whether you possess a large investment portfolio or only some change at the bottom of your purse, care for your money as the gift of God that it is.

[Jesus said:] "Whoever is faithful in a very little is faithful also in much."

Luke 16:10 NRSV

TOUCH A LIFE

Do not repay evil with evil or insult with insult, but with blessing, because to this you were called so that you may inherit a blessing.

1 Peter 3:9 NIV

hink of a woman who has touched your life in a particular way. She may have shown you a special kindness or helped you during a difficult time in your life, choosing to devote her time to you in the midst of everything else vying for her attention.

Being a blessing to others means you put their needs before your own, gladly and willingly listening, helping, and comforting. You may hear a thank-you at the time, or only later when the person realizes how much you helped, or maybe not at all—but you will certainly hear it from the lips of Jesus, who works through you to bless the lives of others.

> Become the kind of container God can use to present any and every kind of gift to his guests for their blessing.
>
> 2 Timothy 2:21 THE MESSAGE

Dear God: Wherever my day takes me, grant that I may touch lives for good. As you have blessed me, I have resolved to bless others. Amen.

211

RESTING IN HIM

[Jesus said]: "Don't worry. . . . Your heavenly Father already knows all your needs."

Matthew 6:31–32 NLT

uring his earthly ministry, Jesus enjoyed visiting the home of sisters Mary and Martha. One visit found Martha so anxious about getting the meal ready she paid scant attention to Jesus! The story reminds us not to let concern over petty details rob us of life's true delights.

When you, like Martha's sister Mary, sit at Jesus' feet and listen to him, your priorities and responsibilities fall into their proper place. Turn your eyes to the God who gives you the skills, abilities, and resources you require to effectively handle whatever situation arises in your life. He knows what you need today, tomorrow, and forever.

Do not worry about anything, but in everything by prayer and supplication with thanksgiving let your requests be made known to God.

Philippians 4:6 NRSV

Heavenly Father: Help me follow Mary's example, and keep me secure in the knowledge that you will take care of all my needs. Amen.

AN INTERDEPENDENT PURPOSE

How good and how pleasant it is for brethren to dwell together in unity!

Psalm 133:1 AMP

It's God's desire that harmony be a characteristic of his people. Unfortunately, sometimes the church becomes confused about how to go about achieving it. Instead of striving for authentic unity, it settles for uniformity—a human understanding of what the church should look like. This falls short of God's will.

Rather, there is only one way to be truly unified, and that is for each person to be wholeheartedly obedient to God. God never contradicts himself, so when everyone is doing as he says, they're actually working toward the same goal—an interdependent purpose—whether they realize it or not.

> *God, I pray that my church would be devoted to serving you wholeheartedly—so that we would have the peace, harmony, and unity that glorify you. Amen.*

Therefore, friend, realize that the best way for you to preserve the harmony of the church is to focus your heart, soul, mind, and strength on God. He will take care of the rest.

The Lord has promised to bless his people with life forevermore.

Psalm 133:3 CEV

HEART'S PEACE

Peacemakers who sow in peace raise a harvest of righteousness.

James 3:18 NIV

Though you may not be in a position to call an end to all wars, God still places on you the mantle of peacemaker. God knows true peace begins in the human heart, so he grants you his peace and the insight you need to live in harmony with who you are and the life he has given you. To make peace with the past, you have his forgiveness, and to know peace today and every day, you possess his strength and wisdom.

Your deep conviction of God's peace works harmony among those around you. There's something about peace that catches on, one heart at a time.

How beautiful upon the mountains are the feet of the messenger who announces peace.

Isaiah 52:7 NRSV

Heavenly Father: Help me know your peace even in the midst of struggle. Grant me harmony of heart and soul so I can become your instrument of peace. Amen.

BUOYED BY PRAYER

Don't burn out; keep yourselves fueled and aflame. Be alert servants of the Master, cheerfully expectant. Don't quit in hard times; pray all the harder.

Romans 12:11–12 THE MESSAGE

rayer is essential to a solid relationship with God. How well would athletes do, how much could they achieve, without constant dialogue with the coach? God, through his Holy Spirit, is your coach. He will provide you with encouragement, instruction, and inspiration. And he will be constantly looking out for your interests as well.

Don't hesitate to tell your coach what you need, and be quick to do what he asks of you. After all, his goal is victory in your life. If you listen to him, he can help you avoid burnout and stay motivated to accomplish great things. Like good teammates, pray together, and share the lessons you learn with each other. Work together for that big win!

God, thank you for coaching me through the great race of life. Challenge me to reach my full potential. Amen.

Get down on your knees before the Master; it's the only way you'll get on your feet.

James 4:10 THE MESSAGE

LOVE FOR HIS WORD

The precepts of the Lord are right, giving joy to the heart.

Psalm 19:8 NIV

Of all the books in the world, none has endured as well or changed as many lives as the Bible. That is because it is God's unique revelation of himself. Through his Word and his Spirit within you, you get to know your Creator, you are able to receive his comfort and direction, and you discover how to live a life that is pleasing to him.

Are you reading the psalms as you are reading this devotional? Are they blessing your heart and illuminating your soul? God wants to give you joy through this wonderful love letter he has inspired for your edification. Therefore, embrace this treasure trove of wisdom and allow him to change your life through it. Certainly it is the best book you will ever read.

God, I praise you for your wonderful Word. Create a love for your precepts and promises in me and help me to know you better through it. Amen.

The judgments of the Lord are true; they are completely right. They are worth more than gold, even the purest gold. They are sweeter than honey, even the finest honey. By them your servant is warned. Keeping them brings great reward.

Psalm 19:9–11 NCV

OUT OF THE DEEP

He reached down from on high and took hold of me; He pulled me out of deep waters.

2 Samuel 21:17 HCSB

*D*ifficult days come unexpectedly—like a flood. You cannot plan for them; neither can you prepare for how they affect you. Though outside, unexpected forces may be their cause, they mainly come through the common things of life. It is the abundance of small, daily problems that can inundate your soul.

Even as the waters of adversity rage, remember that God is your great lifeguard and that he is able to rescue you. Turn each problem—each drowning drop of difficulty—over to him every day. Surely he will lift you out of the overwhelming waters and bring you out to a spacious place where you can breathe.

> He brought me out to a wide-open place;
> He rescued me because He delighted in me.
>
> 2 Samuel 21:20 HCSB

God, thank you for rescuing me out of any deep wave of difficulty that comes my way. I truly delight in you. Amen.

Call upon Me in the day
of trouble; I shall rescue you,
and you will honor Me.

PSALM 50:15 NASB

GOD'S FAMILY

Encourage the oppressed. Defend the cause of the fatherless, plead the case of the widow.

Isaiah 1:17 NIV

She has no one but me to help her," the woman said, "and I'm afraid I'll end up the same way." The single woman pictured herself alone and helpless, but she was forgetting one undeniable fact—she belonged to God's family.

Your relationship with God puts you in direct relationship with others who love him. With the privilege of relationship comes the responsibility to be sensitive to the needs of those in your circle. The same is true for your friends in the faith, for in your time of need you have not only the right but the obligation to ask them to help you. It's what family is for.

Dear God:
Motivate me to help those in my faith family who need assistance, and help me to be willing to receive from others in my own time of need.
Amen.

Whenever we have an opportunity, let us work for the good of all, and especially for those of the family of faith.

Galatians 6:10 NRSV

PURPOSE THROUGH FORGIVENESS

Wash away all my guilt and make me clean again. . . . Then I will teach your ways to those who do wrong, and sinners will turn back to you.

Psalm 51:2, 13 NCV

If you have ever asked God to forgive your sin, then you know how much relief it brings. Released from your transgressions, you were no longer oppressed by the stress and guilt they caused you. Rather, you were transformed into a new creation with a clean, peaceful heart and you regained your hopefulness for a bright future.

Hopefully you are not enjoying your liberty alone.

You see, people need hope—they are longing to find the same forgiveness you have been so graciously given.

So today, tell others about God's forgiveness and salvation so they can be liberated from their sin and experience his peace. It is too wonderful a message to keep to yourself, so share it with everyone you know.

> Save me from bloodguilt, O God, the God who saves me, and my tongue will sing of your righteousness.
>
> Psalm 51:14 NIV

God, I praise you for your astounding forgiveness. Help me to tell others about your salvation so that they can enjoy the same freedom that you have given to me. Amen.

LOOK AND SEE

It is not those who commend themselves that are approved, but those whom the Lord commends.

2 Corinthians 10:18 NRSV

*S*ome women spend a considerable amount of time in front of the mirror each morning, while others may only take a quick glance at themselves before dashing out the door. Perhaps you're somewhere in between. No matter how—or how long—you look at yourself, God is the one who sees you clearly.

Dear God: You know me better than I know myself, and you love me. Let me see myself through the eyes of your love. Amen.

God sees and appreciates your true inner beauty that the mirror doesn't reveal. Because of his unconditional love for you, you need never worry about being enough, doing enough, or achieving enough to earn his approval. You already have it.

Look in the mirror. Ask God to show you the beloved and beautiful woman he sees.

The Lord does not look at the things man looks at. Man looks at the outward appearance, but the Lord looks at the heart.

1 Samuel 16:7 NIV

A PERSONAL RESPONSIBILITY

Defend the weak and the orphans; defend the rights of the poor and suffering.

Psalm 82:3 NCV

The enemy of your soul cannot defeat you—not as long as Jesus is guarding your life. Nothing is more powerful than Christ's ability to sustain you. He is all-knowing and all-powerful. No force on this earth can overwhelm you when you are walking in fellowship with him.

However, when you choose to disobey him and strike out on your own, you will receive only what you can produce. You also will expose yourself to the enemy's sinister attacks.

Jesus promises to defend you and to fight on your behalf, but only if you are surrendered to his manner of protecting you. Therefore, do not put yourself in harm's way. Seek the Savior, who has promised to bless and keep you, because he is faithful to give you the victory.

> Rescue weak and needy people. Help them escape the power of wicked people.
>
> Psalm 82:4 GOD'S WORD

Lord, keep me close to you. Make me aware of my weaknesses so I can surrender them to you. Amen.

WHAT YOUR EYES
TAKE IN

My eyes shall be upon the faithful of the land, that they may dwell with me; He who walks in a blameless way is the one who will minister to me.

Psalm 101:6 NASB

ave you ever experienced that pang of longing in your heart that comes after an especially beautiful love story? Or the grumbling of your stomach after a particularly delectable cooking demonstration? These are small evidences of the effect that the things you watch, read, and listen to have on you.

Whether or not you realize it, the media you allow into your life shapes the way you think and react to situations. If you have been struggling in a particular area, the shows, music, and books you have been partaking of may have contributed to the problem.

God wants to fill you with good things that will bring joy to your soul and strengthen your heart. Therefore, if you think he would disapprove of something that is influencing you—let it go.

God, please show me if there is anything in my life that is influencing me in a negative way. I know that you will always keep me from harm. Amen.

I will ponder the way that is blameless. . . .
I will walk with integrity of heart within my house; I will not set before my eyes anything that is worthless.

Psalm 101:2–3 ESV

LIGHTEN THE LOAD

Do not fear or be dismayed; tomorrow go out against them, for the Lord is with you.

2 Chronicles 20:17 NKJV

Imagine yourself weighed down with several heavy bags of groceries. Just as you realize they're too much for you to manage, a friend comes along to help you. What a relief when she lifts the load from your arms!

When the weight of worry and anxiety burdens your heart, God will be there beside you. With outstretched arms, he lifts your burdens and takes care of them for you. He knows what you're going through, and you can trust him with all the details, big and small. Tell him everything. He will give you the strength and wisdom you need to overcome the hardships you are facing.

Blessed be the Lord, who daily bears our burden.

Psalm 68:19 NASB

God in heaven: Thank you for taking my burdens. With you beside me, I can emerge triumphant from any struggle. Amen.

WORTHY OF A WOMAN'S VOICE

The Lord gave the command; a great company of women brought the good news.

Psalm 68:11 HCSB

esus was very aware of the spiritual devotion of the women who followed him. He knew they were committed to God and wanted to serve him in far greater ways than the social climate of their society allowed. Mary of Bethany sat at his feet listening as he taught God's truth. Her greatest need was satisfied in Christ's presence. She was a true believer—fully committed and determined to worship the Savior.

Shape my life, Lord God. Teach me your ways and your Word. Use me in other people's lives for your glory. And let my life be a psalm of praise to you. Amen.

God uses women to tell others about his power to save and heal the wounds that sin has wrought. Mary soaked up every word spoken to her by the Savior, and you can do the same. When opportunities come, you will be prepared to serve because you have been with the Lord.

Let the godly rejoice. Let them be glad in God's presence. Let them be filled with joy. Sing praises to God and to his name! . . . His name is the Lord—rejoice in his presence!

Psalm 68:3–4 NLT

July 22

FOLLOW
THE LEADER

*[Servants] must be reverent before the mystery of the faith,
not using their position to try to run things.*

1 Timothy 3:9 THE MESSAGE

*M*ore and more women occupy leadership positions in the corporate world, in the community, and in politics. As a child of God, you possess the status of a servant-leader, and the requirements of a leader apply to you.

Leaders step out in front of the crowd instead of worrying about what everyone else is doing, and so must you when you look to God's rules and his expectations. Leaders look beyond today's wants for tomorrow's needs and take responsible action even when subject to the doubts and opposition of others. True servant-leaders live in a way worthy of emulation, and by example, guide others to God.

The Lord will go ahead of you, and he, the God of Israel, will protect you from behind.

Isaiah 52:12 TLB

Dear God: By following you, I am stepping out from the crowd. Grant me your strength and boldness so by my example I can lead others to you. Amen.

A REASON FOR CONFIDENCE

May he give you what you desire and make all your plans succeed.

Psalm 20:4 GNT

Throughout the Bible, you read of people who had amazing challenges but were able to face them with astonishing confidence and assurance. Moses, Joshua, David, and Paul all faced terrible odds but did not falter. How was it possible?

The answer is not found in their strength, but in the might of the One they believed in wholeheartedly. They all trusted God and realized that no matter how bad the situation, he could overcome it.

You should have confidence for the same reason. No matter what God calls you to do, you will see the victory and the wonderful blessings he has for you as long as you obey him. You may not have great earthly resources, but you have God, and he makes you a winner every time.

God, thank you for giving me such a wonderful reason for confidence! Help me to trust you wholeheartedly and obey you always. Amen.

Some trust in their war chariots and others in their horses, but we trust in the power of the Lord our God. Such people will stumble and fall, but we will rise and stand firm.

Psalm 20:7–8 GNT

GOOD NEIGHBOR POLICY

Love your neighbor as yourself.
Leviticus 19:18 NIV

e're right to react with compassion, even anger, when we hear about third-world women and their children living in abject poverty, yet we often find ourselves immune to the many kinds of suffering endured by people living in our own communities.

God directs your eyes toward the needs of all people, particularly those you see every day as you go about your tasks, responsibilities, and recreation; you can have an immediate and a visible impact on the lives and well-being of your closest neighbors. Your nonjudgmental assistance and your willingness to extend yourself for the sake of making their lives better places you on the path to true happiness.

Never walk away from someone who deserves help; your hand is God's hand for that person.

Proverbs 3:28 THE MESSAGE

Heavenly Father: Teach me to see others as you see them so I will do everything in my power to help them, encourage them, and forge productive and harmonious relationships. Amen.

FROM BARREN TO FRUITFUL

*He grants the barren woman a home, like a joyful mother of children.
Praise the Lord!*

Psalm 113:9 NKJV

Rejoice that God always provides exactly what you need. Even if you long for children, but haven't had any, don't fret. God has a marvelous plan for you.

It all hinges on maintaining the right attitude. Set a goal to become involved in the lives of others—especially young people, who will remember you as a godly role model.

God, there are times when I doubt your purpose, especially when it involves my desires. Give me insight into your will so I can rejoice in all you have given me. Amen.

Years ago a young woman established a school for students who didn't have the financial ability to attend college. She believed all students should become all God wanted them to be. Years later students continue to remember this woman's commitment to their future. While she never had children of her own, there is an army of young people who saw her as a caring and godly surrogate mother.

She was exactly what they needed, just as you can be.

He raises the poor from the dust; he lifts the needy from their misery and makes them companions of princes.

Psalm 113:7–8 GNT

A MESSAGE FROM CREATION

What a wildly wonderful world, God! You made it all, with Wisdom at your side, made earth overflow with your wonderful creations.

Psalm 104:24 THE MESSAGE

There will be times when life feels a little flat and even dull. You start your daily routine and find yourself wondering why your attitude toward it has changed. Was there a time when it felt special and enjoyable?

Everyone feels this way at some point—it is as if life has lost its luster. However, there is a solution: Recall the awesome, creative power of God—surveying his handiwork and enjoying the world he has designed. The psalmist realized that when he praised God for his wondrous works, his heart lifted to new heights.

You can do the same. Discover fresh hope for your day and expectancy for the future by remembering all the awesome things God has done.

God, please draw me near to you today so that I may see you and your creation in a new way. Truly you are infinite in nature and loving in all your ways. Amen.

> I will sing to the Lord as long as I live; I will sing praise to my God while I have my being. May my meditation be sweet to Him; I will be glad in the Lord.

Psalm 104:33–34 NKJV

READY TO RENEW

Wipe out all that I have done wrong. Create a clean heart in me, O God, and renew a faithful spirit within me.

Psalm 51:9–10 GOD'S WORD

salm 51 records David's repentance for committing adultery with Bathsheba and murdering her husband. It is the profoundly moving prayer of a man devastated by the depth of his sin. Yet in the midst of his despair, he clung to the love and grace of God and refused to let go.

God, thank you for forgiving my sin and renewing my relationship with you. I cling to your love and rejoice in your wonderful mercy. Amen.

Perhaps you have been shocked at the temptations that have seized your own heart. You may have even fallen in sin, and your spirit is as broken as David's was. Remember, friend, just as God forgave and restored David, he will forgive and restore you if you will confess your sin and repent.

Do not lose hope. Rather, cling to God. Trust him, and he will not only cleanse your heart, but he will renew your spirit as well.

Restore the joy of your salvation to me, and provide me with a spirit of willing obedience. . . . O God, you do not despise a broken and sorrowful heart.

Psalm 51:12, 17 GOD'S WORD

July 28

HEART OF MERCY

[God's] mercy goes on from generation to generation, to all who reverence him.

Luke 1:50 TLB

An act of mercy includes offering practical help to people in need, but it doesn't end there. God set the standard for mercy when he embraced humanity with a heart of compassion and tender care.

God's mercy on you means you have his protection, his forgiveness, and his help for your every need. This is the kind of compassion he models for you to show others, a compassion marked by attentive care for the needs of others, unconditional pardon for the offenses of others, and quiet forgiveness for the omissions of others.

Your heart of compassion should pour out mercy with unreserved generosity.

[Jesus said:] "Have mercy, just as your Father has mercy."

Luke 6:36 NIrV

Heavenly Father: Let your continuing compassion motivate my words, acts, and attitude of mercy toward others, especially the weak and needy. Amen.

TIME IS HIS TOOL

It is time to be gracious to her, for the appointed time has come.

Psalm 102:13 NASB

*D*o you ever feel as if time is your enemy? There is either too little of it when deadlines assail, or too much when waiting for some blessed hope. Yet understand—time is not your foe. Rather, it is a precision instrument that God uses in your life to develop your potential.

Through abbreviated seasons—when there isn't enough time to get everything done—he shows you his mighty wisdom, power, and mercy. During the long years of waiting—while every emotion is tested—he molds your faith and character.

Time isn't your enemy, friend. Time is merely a tool in God's hand to reveal himself to you in a new way. His grace is sufficient for every moment of your life—so trust him and look to him *whenever* you are in need.

God, even though time is a driving factor in my life, I thank you that I don't have to fear it. I praise you for your lovingkindness every moment of every day. Amen.

Long ago you laid the foundation of the earth. Even the heavens are the works of your hands. They will come to an end, but . . . you remain the same, and your life will never end.

Psalm 102:25–27 GOD'S WORD

MENDING WOUNDS

*The Lord . . . has sent me to bring good news to the oppressed,
to bind up the brokenhearted.*

Isaiah 61:1 NRSV

"If I can stop one heart from breaking," Emily Dickinson wrote, "I shall not live in vain."

The poet knew that the key to a rewarding life is to focus not on our own comfort but on the comfort and happiness of others. Each day you "stop one heart from breaking" by listening attentively to the voice of another, hearing what that one says, and being sensitive to those things only suggested in a look, a shrug, or a sigh. Your willingness to empathize and extend yourself on the behalf of another, even at the price of inconvenience to you, guarantees you "shall not live in vain."

Dear God: Grant me a heart like yours— filled with compassion and always ready to receive those who weep and whose spirits cry out for consolation. Amen.

[God] heals the brokenhearted.

Psalm 147:3 NCV

OF PRAISE AND POWER

Be exalted, Lord, in Your strength; we will sing and praise Your power.

Psalm 21:13 AMP

Allow the words to roll from your lips, "Lord, I praise your wonderful power." Say the phrase aloud, "My God, I trust your faultless strength."

Is this exercise of adoration difficult for you today? Is there an issue weighing on your heart that prevents you from adoring the Lord? If so, it is even more essential for you to turn your thoughts away from your suffering and to his sufficiency, to replace the pain of your trials with the reality of his triumph.

Worship the Lord, who can and will help you. Rejoice and be glad that he is with you and will never fail. It is when you refocus your attention on him that you will see victory as a possibility. That, friend, is the true power of praise.

God, I want to trust you—so I will praise you with an open heart. I rejoice in your faultless strength and know your mighty hand will provide the victory. Amen.

You have granted him the desire of his heart and have not withheld the request of his lips. You welcomed him with rich blessings.

Psalm 21:2–3 NIV

AUGUST

Regardless of what else you put on, wear love. It's your basic, all-purpose garment. Never be without it.

COLOSSIANS 3:14 THE MESSAGE

ALONE

When I look beside me, I see that there is no one to help me, no one to protect me. . . . Lord, I cry to you for help; you, Lord, are my protector; you are all I want in this life.

Psalm 142:4–5 GNT

here are struggles that are so deep and hurt so badly that you cannot share them with someone else. Uncertainty, insecurity, hurt, fear, shame, and confusion cloak your situation in darkness, hindering you from bringing the issue into the light of another's love and counsel. The loneliness of this area infects your whole life, and soon enough the feeling of alienation consumes you.

God, I recognize that I need your healing, but it's difficult to let go of this painful issue. Please help me. Thank you for not abandoning me in this area of need. Amen.

You're not alone, and this issue is not too awful for God to deal with. He knows that it's debilitating you from experiencing his best for your life.

It's scary, but you must allow him to illuminate the situation so that he can set you free of the prison it has become to you. He is already working in you, so don't go through this alone. Trust him.

Set me free from my prison, that I may praise your name. Then the righteous will gather about me because of your goodness to me.

Psalm 142:7 NIV

GOD'S VICTORY OVER SELF-DEFEAT

*My sins, O God, are not hidden from you; you know how fool-
ish I have been. Don't let me bring shame on those who trust in
you, Sovereign Lord Almighty!*

Psalm 69:5–6 GNT

hen you become aware of your potential to stray from God's love, you may feel shocked and even disappointed. Temptations can entangle you, and sin can settle deep within your heart—preventing you from enjoying a close relationship with God.

It is easy to spot the signs of spiritual compromise in your life—you justify the sin and temptation, feel that you need to rush about rather than rest in God's presence, and give God and others a list of excuses about why your devotion is off course.

Nothing is more important than your relationship with him. In addition, when you lay aside your sin and go to him with a heart of devotion, you will notice a difference. Your life will be marked by peace and joy.

O God, in the greatness of Your loving-kindness, answer me with Your saving truth. . . . The humble have seen it and are glad; you who seek God, let your heart revive.

Psalm 69:13, 32 NASB

*God, I know my
tendency to self-
destruct through sin
and moral compromise.
Please keep me from
straying in my love
toward you. Amen.*

HUMBLED

My heart is not proud, O Lord. . . . I do not concern myself with great matters or things too wonderful for me. But I have stilled and quieted my soul.

Psalm 131:1–2 NIV

There's a pride problem whenever you imagine that you know better than God does. Unfortunately, it's an easy trap to fall into. From your point of view, you know exactly how things should work out. You pray and tell God your plans and how you would like everything to fall into place.

But God says, "No" or "Wait." It frustrates you.

Friend, you don't know better than God does because your perspective is limited. You have absolutely no idea about what's ahead or what he has in mind.

Therefore, whenever you start to believe you've got your plans all figured out—stop. Back up. Humble yourself before him and acknowledge that he is the One in control. Because "God resists the proud, but gives grace to the humble" (James 4:6 GNT).

God, I acknowledge that I've tried to wrestle control from your omnipotent hand. Please forgive me. Teach me to humbly accept your will. Amen.

Hope in the Lord from this time forth and forever.

Psalm 131:3 AMP

THE GOD OF SECOND CHANCES

The Lord helps the fallen and lifts up those bent beneath their loads.

Psalm 145:14 NLT

It would be great if we could live our lives perfectly, always making good, appropriate choices. We can't, because we have free will—a priceless gift from God. He wants us to have a loving relationship with him because we choose to, not because we were designed to.

The risk of free will is that we often choose wrongly. God knew we would and paid for our mistakes ahead of time. In return, he only wants us to ask to be forgiven. He has promised not to deny our request. Why be burdened with your mistakes? You can lay them down at the feet of the God of Second Chances.

Heavenly Father: Thank you for freely granting me the right to choose. And forgive me for the wrong choices I have made. Amen.

Lord, you are kind and forgiving and have great love for those who call to you.

Psalm 86:5 NCV

LIVING WELL

Let each of you look not to your own interests, but to the interests of others.

Philippians 2:4 NRSV

If you're in the working world, you've probably been advised to look out for your own interests first, because no one else will. If you've been following God's way, for even a short time, however, you already know he turns the advice upside down and says, "Put the interests of others before your own."

Dear God: Help me turn my attention to others, keeping in mind the consequences my words and actions have on the lives of those around me. Amen.

God's Spirit opens the way for you to consider how your decisions affect others and whether or not you want to carry out a particular plan, given the consequences your actions are likely to have on the lives of others.

Not everyone will understand why you don't put yourself first, but God will.

Love isn't selfish.

1 Corinthians 13:5 CEV

THE BALM OF THANKSGIVING

"Bring your thanks to God as a sacrifice, and keep your vows to the Most High. Call on me in times of trouble. I will rescue you, and you will honor me."

Psalm 50:14–15 GOD'S WORD

The Bible encourages you to give thanks to God in every situation, even in the circumstances that are difficult. This shows your willingness to have faith in him even in the most trying areas of your life.

Yet perhaps as you are expressing your gratefulness, you find that there are experiences and troubles that you just cannot trust him with. The wounds are too deep and the sacrifice too painful.

Friend, God understands. Yet he does not ask for gratitude for his sake. He does it to make you whole. He knows that when you praise him, it exposes the hidden injuries of your heart to his healing touch.

Therefore, friend, thank him, even when it is a sacrifice. His loving restoration is something you can truly be grateful for.

He who sacrifices thank offerings honors me, and he prepares the way so that I may show him the salvation of God.

Psalm 50:23 NIV

My God, you know how difficult this is for me. This area is so painful. Yet I will trust your loving touch. Thank you for healing me, my precious Lord. Amen.

August 7

ROLE MODEL

Be an example to the believers with your words, your actions, your love, your faith, and your pure life.

1 Timothy 4:12 NCV

In our formative years, the women we chose as role models influenced how we perceived ourselves and the goals we set for ourselves. Now, as adults, we are the ones younger women watch.

God reminds you that your appearance and behavior matter, because he understands how influential you are to those around you, especially young women who are still discovering their own personalities and priorities. As a role model, the way you carry yourself reflects your values, and the words you use in everyday conversation declare your attitude toward God and other people.

Dear God: Help me conduct myself in a manner worthy of emulation, especially for those in need of an example of godly womanhood. Amen.

You were created not only to please God but also to reflect his virtue and demonstrate his goodness and purity.

In all things show them how to live by your life.

Titus 2:7 NLV

TROUBLESOME ATTRACTIONS

Take away my desire to do evil or to join others in doing wrong.

Psalm 141:4 NCV

No one denies that temptations are truly tempting! The promise of immediate gratification will always be dangerous as long as you live on this earth.

How do you stop falling prey to the things that lure you into sin? You know Jesus has already broken the power of sin over you, but why is it still so attractive to you? How do you stop *wanting* the things that harm you?

Romans 12:2 (NLT) instructs, "Let God transform you into a new person by changing the way you think." Temptation begins in your thoughts; you must therefore change what you set your mind on.

Focus on God, and allow him to cleanse you with the Bible. Those troublesome temptations will not go away immediately, but over time, you will find that your desire to do wrong will certainly diminish.

> *God, I know that I have often focused on the very things that make me stumble and sin. Transform me, God, because I want to honor you with my whole life. Amen.*

My eyes are upon You, O God the Lord; in You I take refuge.

Psalm 141:8 NKJV

BY THE LIGHT
OF HIS FACE

We shall not turn back from you; give us life, and we will call upon your name! Restore us, O Lord God of hosts! Let your face shine, that we may be saved!

Psalm 80:18–19 ESV

About Jesus, John 1:4–5 (NLT) reports, "His life brought light to everyone. The light shines in the darkness, and the darkness can never extinguish it." The light of God's love and salvation can never be quenched.

Lord, illuminate my life with your unquenchable love and hope. I praise you that all fear and darkness flees when your light shines on my heart. Amen.

When you are lonely, draw near to the Lord and he will brighten your day. When sorrow tries to settle in around you and tempt you to feel discouraged, lost, or forgotten, read his Word and ask him to illuminate your life. He will do it—he will speak to your heart and remind you that you are not alone.

When you encounter emotional clouds or rain, take a moment to ask God to light your way with his everlasting hope. He always answers the prayers of his children.

O Shepherd of Israel . . . You who dwell between the cherubim, shine forth!

Psalm 80:1 NKJV

REMEMBER TO RECYCLE

I am the Lord; those who hope in me will not be disappointed.
Isaiah 49:23 NIV

If you recycle, you've asked yourself this question: "How can I use this instead of throwing it away?" When life lets you down, you might imagine God asking you, "Beloved woman, how can we turn this setback into something good and useful?"

When you turn your eyes to him, your setback will become experience and serve as a useful reminder to look forward in faith to the next opportunity he offers you. It will serve to keep you mindful of his providential care, and it will prepare you to explore, discover, and pursue great things.

Use and reuse your experiences, and he will turn disappointments into victories.

None of those who wait for You will be ashamed.

Psalm 25:3 NASB

Dear God: You have excellent plans for me, and I know all your plans will work out for my good and well-being. Amen.

A RECORD OF RESCUE

*Our ancestors trusted you. They trusted, and you rescued them.
They cried to you and were saved. They trusted you and were never
disappointed.*

Psalm 22:4–5 GOD'S WORD

Hundreds of prophecies throughout the Old Testament predicted the coming of the One who would deliver people from their sins. Psalm 22 contains some of the particulars about the Messiah, and almost a thousand years after it was written those details came true in the person of Jesus Christ.

Jesus is not only the Savior; he is also living proof that the Lord keeps *all* of his promises. Although Psalm 22 is a difficult passage to read, it is also a wonderful reminder that all who trust in him are never disappointed.

Therefore, trust the Lord Jesus to save you from your sins and to rescue you in all of your difficult circumstances. You can count on him, because not only is his record the best—it is perfect.

God, you are utterly astounding! Thank you for saving me from my sins and rescuing me from my troubles. Truly you are worthy of all my praise! Amen.

In the midst of the assembly I will praise You. You who fear the Lord, praise Him!

Psalm 22:22–23 NKJV

HEART OF PEACE

*Live in harmony by showing love for each other. Be united in
what you think, as if you were only one person.*

Philippians 2:2 CEV

In any relationship, a time comes when you and the
other person disagree. In the Bible, God offers a way
to handle the situation so your relationship remains strong, healthy, and vibrant.

It pleases God when you willingly
promote harmony and peace. Consider
being the one who chooses not to take
offense at the carelessly spoken remark,
or being the first to point out those things
the two of you agree on and the value of
your relationship. Imagine the outcome if
you were always to care more about the
other person than about winning. Strive for peace, and see how all
your relationships strengthen, deepen, and endure.

*Heavenly Father:
Put in me a peaceful
heart, and teach me
to choose my words
carefully when I am
in difficult situations.
Amen.*

It's a mark of good character to avert quarrels.

Proverbs 20:3 THE MESSAGE

THE SONG OF YOUR LIFE

Come, praise the Lord, all his servants.
Psalm 134:1 GNT

There are certain tunes that immediately stir your soul. The music is uplifting, the lyrics inspiring, and for some reason it touches your heart whenever you hear it.

There are some people who have the same effect on your life. A smile spreads across your face whenever you see them, and a sweet melody of faith, kindness, and joy follows them even during the most difficult times. They've set their heart on God—and it resonates to all who know them.

What does your life tell people about God? Do you inspire others to follow him?

Is your life a praise hymn—or a dirge? An overture of peace and trust—or a lament of pain and tragedy?

You can choose the tune. What will the song of your life be?

Lift up your hands to the holy place and bless the Lord!

Psalm 134:2 ESV

God, I want my life to be a song of worship and thanksgiving to you! Please show me how to be a person of praise. May all who meet me want to know you. Amen.

ETERNAL PLEDGE

All the promises of God in Him are Yes, and in Him Amen, to the glory of God through us.

2 Corinthians 1:20 NKJV

"I promise." The intent of those words, when uttered this side of heaven, sometimes falls short. When uttered by God, those two words point to an unbreakable and unchanging pledge you can rely on.

At the heart of God's many pledges throughout the Bible is his commitment to you and your eternal life with him. When God presented Jesus to take your place on the cross, he confirmed his vow to offer salvation to you and all people. His Spirit's work in your life right now shows God cares for you and waits for you to accept the many marvelous promises he has made.

> *Heavenly Father: Your promises amaze and humble me. It is my privilege and pleasure to receive your magnificent gifts. Amen.*

The Lord is faithful in all his words, and gracious in all his deeds.

Psalm 145:13 NRSV

I NEED YOU RIGHT NOW!

I am poor and needy; make haste to me, O God! You are my help and my deliverer; O Lord, do not delay.

Psalm 70:5 NKJV

Have you ever noticed that sometimes when you try your hardest to make something work, it turns out wrong? These are often the times when God allows you to face difficulty in order to teach you to trust him more deeply.

By spending time with him in prayer—listing your concerns, desires, and needs—you are telling him that you need him. Nothing touches his heart more profoundly than hearing your sincere prayer: "Father God, I can't do this on my own. I need you." Such humility immediately stirs his compassion.

Friend, always remember that you can reach your goals by keeping your heart set on him. So call to him. He is certainly ready to respond and will send the wisdom you need for success.

Let all who love your saving way say over and over, "God is mighty!"

Psalm 70:4 THE MESSAGE

God, I know there are times when I rush ahead of you. I'm sorry. I confess my need and ask you to step into my situation so I will have your infinite support. Amen.

WORTHY VENTURES

My mouth shall speak wisdom; the meditation of my heart shall be understanding. I will incline my ear to a proverb.

Psalm 49:3–4 ESV

As a beloved child of God, there are some activities that are not worthy of your time. Pursuing possessions that quickly perish, holding grudges, fretting over the future, and achieving ambitions by unjust means are all deeds that are unbecoming to one who belongs to the Lord.

Friend, you have goals more significant to accomplish. Strengthening your relationship with God through prayer and Bible study, representing him faithfully in the world, being a good example, and telling others about him so they can be freed from sin are all exercises that have enduring results in eternity.

God, I want to honor you. Please show me the activities that merit my time and the ones that do not so I can glorify you with my entire life. Amen.

You are a woman of worth, so do not waste your precious life on unworthy pursuits. Rather, do only things that honor God. Then you can be sure that every minute is time well spent.

See what happens to those who trust in themselves, the fate of those who are satisfied with their wealth—they are doomed. . . . But God will rescue me; he will save me from the power of death.

Psalm 49:13–15 GNT

JUST MEANS TO AN END

Defend the rights of the poor and needy.

Proverbs 31:9 NIV

he history of women and their role in society makes us especially attuned to the plight of those who find themselves powerless because of factors beyond their control, such as age, gender, ethnicity, or economic status.

Dear God:
Thank you for
allowing me to reflect
your care for the needy
through the things I
can do for those who
struggle against
injustice. Amen.

You help loose the bonds of injustice when you take a firm stand against it, beginning with the opinions you harbor, the conversations you join, and the way you treat weak and vulnerable people. You continue by volunteering in your community and pledging your support to responsible charities.

God loves the poor and needy, regardless of how they came to be poor and needy. He wants to use your hands and heart to convey his love and concern.

A good woman is hard to find. . . . She's quick to assist anyone in need, reaches out to help the poor.

Proverbs 31:10, 20 THE MESSAGE

August 18

BONDS OF FRIENDSHIP

A true friend is closer than your own family.
Proverbs 18:24 CEV

ou are blessed indeed if you have a friend you can call in a time of crisis and know she will be there for you. She is the kind of friend God intends for you, and the kind of friend he empowers you to be as well.

True companionship and friendship develops as you go out of your way to support and comfort others. Your constancy allows others to place their trust in you, and your sharing of thoughtfulness, helpfulness, and a listening ear forge the bonds of genuine and lasting friendship.

God has called himself your friend, and he has opened the blessing of friendship to you.

A friend loves at all times. [She is] there to help when trouble comes.

Proverbs 17:17 NIrV

Dear God:
Thank you for the gift of friendship. Help me to be an attentive and appreciative friend, especially when I'm called on to help in a time of need. Amen.

DEEP ROOTS

They are strong, like a tree planted by a river. The tree produces fruit in season, and its leaves don't die. Everything they do will succeed.

Psalm 1:3 NCV

*L*ooking for peace in the Psalms is not a random choice on your part. There's a reason you've come here. Perhaps you're seeking understanding in a difficult situation. Or maybe you don't know where else to turn. Either way, you're looking in the right place—the only place peace can be found: in God. You'll always find God in his Word.

Like river waters nourishing a tree's roots, when you drink in God's Word, it goes deep into your heart and makes you strong. God's nurturing truth gives you the courage and wisdom for whatever you're facing.

God, I know that I haven't come here by chance. Thank you that the Psalms will strengthen my heart and nourish my soul. Amen.

So seek him—allow his Word to take root deep in your heart. You'll be sure to find the peace you're looking for.

Delight in doing everything the Lord wants; day and night . . . think about his law.

Psalm 1:2 NLT

THE SHEPHERD'S REPUTATION

He renews my soul. He guides me along the paths of righteousness for the sake of his name.

Psalm 23:3 GOD'S WORD

One can generally deduce the skill of the shepherd by the condition of his sheep. Is the flock cared for? Healthy, well-fed, free of parasites and injuries? This is due to the shepherd's watchful leadership. He nurtures his lambs with skill and understanding and gladly gives his life to rescue them from danger.

The same is true for your shepherd—the Lord God. He nourishes your soul through his Word and Spirit. He protects you from paths that would destroy you, and exercises your faith so you can grow strong and healthy. He guides you through the perils of life to places of peace.

How well you are cared for reflects on his name, so he is not going to let you down. Therefore, trust the Shepherd. With him, you shall surely never want.

> The Lord is my shepherd; I have everything I need. . . . I know that your goodness and love will be with me all my life; and your house will be my home as long as I live.
>
> *Psalm 23:1, 6 GNT*

Lord, you are my wonderful shepherd. Thank you for leading me so faithfully. May my life bring praise to your good, holy, and merciful name. Amen.

August 21

HEART'S TREASURES

Be diligent to present yourself approved to God, a worker who does not need to be ashamed, rightly dividing the word of truth.

2 Timothy 2:15 NKJV

In the scriptural account of Jesus' birth, we read how his mother, Mary, took in all the signs and wonders around her and treasured them in her heart.

Dear God: Help me become a faithful student of your Word by instilling in me a heart ready and eager to treasure your eternal truths. Amen.

God invites you to treasure his Word in your heart by becoming a student of the Bible. The Bible opens his signs and wonders to you, and diligent study opens your heart to his treasures. Bible literacy is an important element of your walk with God. Through it, you will discover the deeper meanings in Scripture as you see how each piece fits together to assure you of his love, forgiveness, and salvation found in Jesus.

Great peace have they who love your law, and nothing can make them stumble.

Psalm 119:165 NIV

READIED FOR WHATEVER IS AHEAD

I praise you, Lord! You are my mighty rock, and you teach me how to fight my battles.

Psalm 144:1 CEV

It's possible that something you are facing right now has left you reeling in confusion. You've been obedient to God and are serving him faithfully, so this new ordeal makes absolutely no sense. You are utilizing spiritual muscles that are unfamiliar and aching. Everything you believe about him is being stretched and tried in a manner you haven't experienced before.

Whether you realize it or not, you are in training. God is preparing you for important battles ahead, for the tough challenges you will face. The difficulty you are enduring is crucial to making you ready for them.

God, I thank you for readying me for the challenges ahead through this situation. I know you can use it for my good and your glory. Help me to trust you. Amen.

Do not despair! God is using this situation for your good. When you see the wonderful strengths and graces he develops in you through it, you'll surely have cause to praise him.

Blessed are the people whose God is the Lord!

Psalm 144:15 ESV

JOYFUL WAITING

May the God of hope fill you with all joy and peace in believing, that you may abound in hope by the power of the Holy Spirit.

Romans 15:13 NKJV

The prophetess Anna was a devout woman who spent her long widowhood in joyful expectation of the promised redeemer. God rewarded her with the privilege of seeing the infant Jesus and recognizing him as Savior. Anna gave God heartfelt thanks and praise.

When you read and meditate on God's promises to you, he offers you the motivation to live in joyful expectation of their fulfillment. His Spirit, a Spirit of hope, empowers you to rely on what God has already accomplished in your life and to patiently wait on things not yet seen.

In joyful expectation as you await the fruition of his promises, give him heartfelt thanks and praise.

Heavenly Father: The wondrous promises you have made known to me in your Word create a spirit of joyful expectation in me. Amen.

Let praise cascade off my lips; after all, you've taught me the truth about life!

Psalm 119:172 THE MESSAGE

COMMITTED TO PEACE

As far as it depends on you, live at peace with everyone.

Romans 12:18 NIV

The Bible's instruction is that you strive to live in harmony with God's plan and with others. Don't worry; God knows your differences are great. And still, he urges you to do all you can. That means that the humble mind and tender heart you call to bear on your closest relationships must also be extended to others.

Of course, it won't be possible to be in unity with everyone. That's just the way it is. God asks only that you do your part and leave the rest to him. Focus instead on those who have surrendered their lives to the truth of the Bible.

In everything set them an example by doing what is good.

Titus 2:7 NIV

God, it my our desire to live in harmony with those around me. Strike all pride, all prejudice, and unrighteous judgment from my life. Amen.

UNSURPASSED SATISFACTION

Praise the Lord, O my soul, and forget not all his benefits . . . who satisfies your desires with good things so that your youth is renewed like the eagle's.

Psalm 103:2, 5 NIV

A soul can only tolerate stress and self-denial for so long. When challenges or hardships consume you for a prolonged period of time, you must somehow quench the longings within that you've been neglecting.

At times that may mean acting out in a way that is negative—through binge eating, overspending, destructive relationships, substance abuse, or compulsive behaviors. Unfortunately, your reckless actions do nothing to fulfill you and leave you feeling more out of control and discontented than before.

God, help me to focus on you instead of turning to impulsive behaviors that harm me. Only you can truly soothe my soul and alleviate my stress. Amen.

Yet there is a positive way to handle your stress, and that is to spend time alone with God. You will find that he will satisfy you more than anything else ever could. He gives you exactly what you truly need—so always turn to him first.

As the heavens are high above the earth, so great are His mercy and loving-kindness toward those who reverently and worshipfully fear Him.

Psalm 103:11 AMP

JOYOUS TRUTH

The word of the Lord is right, and all His work is done in truth.

Psalm 33:4 NKJV

Joy and happiness are not the same thing. Happiness comes and goes with your circumstances. Sure, it's wonderful while it lasts, but it could be gone in an instant.

Joy, on the other hand, resonates from deep inside as a response to the touch of God. It doesn't fluctuate with external circumstances. Rather, it strengthens you at your core. Joy is a response to certain truths that are unchanging. One such truth is that God loves you. Another is that his forgiveness covers you completely. Still another is that he has endowed you with specific gifts and talents with which to bless yourselves and others. And yet another is that your future is secure in his hands.

> *Dear God, thank you for the joy that comes with recognizing the truth of your presence in my life. Amen.*

What you're after is truth from the inside out. Enter me, then; conceive a new, true life.

Psalm 51:6 THE MESSAGE

NOTHING TO FEAR

Good people will always be remembered. They won't be afraid of bad news; their hearts are steady because they trust the Lord. They are confident and will not be afraid.

Psalm 112:6–8 NCV

When your life is committed to Jesus Christ, you have nothing to fear. Though you face disappointment and hardship, the one thing that never changes is God's love for you. Difficulty comes but you can be certain that he will never fail you.

Why does the opposite seem true at times? Often because the last thing you want to do is deal with the serious problems that confront you. However, God uses adversity to prepare you for greater blessings. He stretches your faith in him—not to harm you, but to teach you to draw near to him.

God, I know the only way I can know you better is by allowing you to teach me what is right. Please give me the strength and courage to follow you always. Amen.

Friend, your trials can either make you bitter or better. Therefore, set your heart on becoming better by drawing near to God and allowing him to work in your life. Determine to stay courageous by focusing on God.

Light arises in the darkness for the upright, gracious, compassionate, and just.

Psalm 112:4 AMP

LIGHT OF DAY

The Lord is near to the brokenhearted, and saves the crushed in spirit.

Psalm 34:18 NRSV

We've all been down in the dumps. Maybe it's just one of those days, or maybe it's more serious than that, but you feel you're in the heart of a dark cloud.

When you encounter one of those days, hold faithfully to prayer. Use prayer to lay out before God the whole of your sadness, even if you have trouble finding the right words. Wrap yourself in the certain knowledge that he hears you and will respond to you with care and concern, sensitivity and understanding. Be patient, even if you do not feel his presence. His light in your life will come as sure as the sun rises each day.

Dear God: Thank you for the knowledge that you are always nearby even when I'm unable to sense the precious gift of your presence. Amen.

I satisfy the weary ones and refresh everyone who languishes.

Jeremiah 31:25 NASB

ETERNITY IN YOUR HEART

As we have heard, so have we seen in the city of the Lord of hosts, in the city of our God; God will establish it forever.

Psalm 48:8 NKJV

oes it ever feel as if you simply do not belong in this world? As if you are longing for something beyond what exists here? You are not imagining things, and you are certainly not alone.

Hebrews 11:13, 16 explains that faithful people throughout the ages have "agreed that they were only strangers and foreigners on this earth. . . . They were looking forward to a better home in heaven" (CEV).

God, thank you for preparing me for heaven. I may not understand it all, but I praise you for establishing a wonderful home for me with you forever. Amen.

You see, when you believe in God, he awakens the desire for eternity in you. Each time you sense that you are out of place here, it is because he's further along in the process of transforming you to live in heaven forever.

Whenever you feel like your heart is somewhere else—that is okay. Just remember, friend, you are not home yet.

This God, our God forever and ever—He will lead us eternally.

Psalm 48:14 HCSB

August 30

A WAY OUT

When you are tempted, he will show you a way out so that you will not give in to it.

1 Corinthians 10:13 NLT

*Y*ou will have temptations today—that is a basic truth of the Christian life. However, just because you have temptations does not mean you will necessarily sin. Just the opposite. Because you have temptations, you have a unique opportunity for success.

The word that Paul used here for *tempted* is also translated as *tested*. These tests can make you stronger if you seek God in them and take the way out he gives you.

Set your heart on God and resolve that you will listen to him when temptation comes your way. He will show you an excellent way out—a way that leads you to victory.

God, thank you for giving me a way of escape from my temptations. Help me always to grow stronger through the tests. Amen.

The Lord knows how to rescue the godly from temptation.

2 Peter 2:9 NASB

LIVING WATER

The Lord will not cast off his people, nor will he forsake his inheritance.

Psalm 94:14 NKJV

The Bible tells of a woman who came to draw water from the community well. For reasons of her own, she chose to come when she would not encounter other women. She didn't worry about the lone man sitting nearby, because he certainly would not speak to her.

But he did speak. Though Jesus knew all about her, he chose instead to look into her heart, and there he found a woman thirsting for true love, compassion, and acceptance.

Jesus came into the world to refresh you with God's strength and assurance, and he welcomes you into his presence. He accepts you just as you are, right to the innermost yearnings of your heart.

Dear God: Thank you for welcoming me with open arms and accepting me just as I am in body, mind, and spirit. Amen.

Jesus replied, "If you only knew the gift God has for you and who I am, you would ask me, and I would give you living water."

John 4:10 NLT

SEPTEMBER

*Let us run with endurance the
race that is set before us, looking
unto Jesus, the author and
finisher of our faith.*

HEBREWS 12:1–2 NKJV

September 1

A PEACEFUL PLACE

It is hard to stop a quarrel once it starts, so don't let it begin.
Proverbs 17:14 TLB

Like many women, you may feel irritable and perhaps even angry. You are certainly not alone in your feelings. More important, you are not distanced from God because you have them. At these times, especially at these times, he offers soothing comfort and nurturing words.

Dear God: In times when I feel my temper flaring, let me run to the cool waters of your calming presence. Amen.

God encourages you to rest with him in his unconditional love. Give him your worries, stresses, aches, and pains. Talk to him about the annoyances that seem to get under your skin at times, and let him heal the wounds of your spirit. Open yourself to his peace, and he will provide it just when you need it most.

The Lord is compassionate and gracious, slow to anger, abounding in love.

Psalm 103:8 NIV

September 2

ACCEPT IT AS A GIFT

*A righteous person may strike me or correct me out of kindness.
It is like lotion for my head. My head will not refuse it, because
my prayer is directed against evil deeds.*

Psalm 141:5 GOD'S WORD

*W*hen a godly person you love and respect confronts you about some fault or failure, it may sting bitterly. Perhaps the anger rises up within you and you're tempted to defend yourself. Or perhaps you wither under her censure—feeling worthless, betrayed, or unloved.

In such moments it is necessary to take a deep breath and refocus on what God is revealing to you through your loved one's words. Is there something God wants you to learn?

The truth can hurt, but if it helps you grow closer to God, then it is truly a gift that is not meant for your harm but for

God, I thank you for my friend and for her honesty to me. God, please show me what you want me to learn from her words, and help me to respond graciously. Amen.

your good. The person who is wise, loving, honest, and courageous enough to confront you about ungodly issues in your life is a finer friend than many.

God, come close. . . . Treat my prayer as sweet incense rising; my raised hands are my evening prayers.

Psalm 141:1–2 THE MESSAGE

GOD'S WAYS

Be merciful to those who doubt.

Jude 22 NIV

Hannah of the Bible was a woman who grieved because she was barren. She prayed deeply for a child, and then, confident in God's willingness to answer, she returned to her daily life. In his own time, God granted her prayer.

Dear God: Guide me through the questions I have, and help me when I need understanding. Lead me to praise the glorious mystery of you. Amen.

Hannah's trust and patience brought her peace, even without proof that God would answer right away. In the same manner, questions of faith and belief often require God's own timing. Uncertainties you bring before him in prayer are addressed and resolved by God as you faithfully watch, wait, and learn of him.

With trust and patience, you will discover God's way in every circumstance and see doubt turned to faith.

Without wavering, let us hold tightly to the hope we say we have, for God can be trusted to keep his promise.

Hebrews 10:23 NLT

PERSONAL TOUCH

A gracious woman retains honor.
Proverbs 11:16 NKJV

*Y*ou know how good it feels when someone you've met only briefly calls you by name, or a friend remembers an event important to you. These kindnesses require time and effort but are guaranteed to bring joy to others and a sense of grace to your life.

Try these simple ways to honor others: Learn and use their names when you are introduced. Write down the dates of friends' birthdays, anniversaries, and other significant information, along with anything you would like to inquire about later. These thoughtful acts will give kindness a starting place in your life and let others know in a real and individual way that you care about them.

Dear God: Just as you know me by name, empower me with a genuine desire to treat others as the unique individuals they are and to show that I care about them. Amen.

Love is patient. Love is kind.
1 Corinthians 13:4 NIrV

FORGET IT

As far as the east is from the west, so far has He removed our transgressions from us.

Psalm 103:12 NKJV

There may be people in your life who never allow you to forget what you have done wrong. Every time you make a mistake, they are quick to pounce—reminding you of the ways you have failed.

However, God isn't like that. Whenever a believer repents he says, "I'll wipe the slate clean. . . . I'll forget they ever sinned!" (Jeremiah 31:34 THE MESSAGE).

Of course, maybe the person who is always reminding you of your faults is . . . you.

Don't do this to yourself. God forgives you, and when he says your sins have been erased forever, there isn't a trace of them left in your life. Therefore, pardon yourself and learn from your errors. Then praise him for all the grace he has shown you.

God, thank you for forgiving all my sins and never reminding me of the way I have failed. You are truly loving and merciful, and I praise you! Amen.

Praise the Lord, my soul, and do not forget how kind he is. He forgives all my sins and heals all my diseases. He keeps me from the grave and blesses me with love and mercy.

Psalm 103:2–4 GNT

BREAKING
DESTRUCTIVE CYCLES

Do not hold us guilty for the sins of our ancestors! Let your compassion quickly meet our needs, for we are on the brink of despair.

Psalm 79:8 NLT

You can change the way you respond to life's trials and temptations, but you cannot do it alone. You need God's encouraging truth to make the switch from failure to success.

Many people think this is impossible. They look at the shortcomings of their parents or other family members and are tempted to think, *I am just like them. I will never change.*

God did not want the nation of Israel to be defeated by the sins of their ancestors. He had a better plan in mind for them. Because of his great love and mercy, they could overcome every obstacle, and you can do the same when you surrender your life to him.

God, I want to be the very best I can be. Therefore, I choose not to dwell on thoughts of defeat or failure. Rather, I rejoice that your life flows through me. Amen.

Then we, your people, the ones you love and care for, will thank you over and over and over. We'll tell everyone we meet how wonderful you are, how praiseworthy you are!

Psalm 79:13 THE MESSAGE

DRYING YOUR TEARS

You will weep no more. He will surely be gracious to you at the sound of your cry; when He hears it, He will answer you.

Isaiah 30:19 AMP

Have you been crying out to God about some dear person or situation? Is there a promise you long for him to fulfill? God will surely be kind and loving to you, and you are absolutely assured that he is going to answer you.

God, it is true that sometimes my faith is weak. Please help me trust in you more, for surely you are already answering my prayers. Amen.

In light of this, ask yourself, Is what draws your tears your own doubt that God will help you? Sometimes your tears are actually evidence that your trust in God must increase.

Take this to heart—God will never, ever fail you. So dry your tears and embrace the peace he longs to give to you. Know that he is absolutely faithful to do as he promised.

I have sought your face with all my heart; be gracious to me according to your promise.

Psalm 119:58 NIV

LOOK FORWARD

Forgetting the past and straining toward what is ahead, I keep trying to reach the goal and get the prize for which God called me through Christ to the life above.

Philippians 3:13–14 NCV

he past cannot be changed," a woman once remarked. "We have only today to make things happen." While well aware of the hold the past can exert over the present, the woman reflected God's wisdom in pointing us forward.

What keeps you looking back? Do hurts, regrets, or grievances from the past take your eyes away from today? If so, let God show you how to let go. Let God help you leave behind the negative thoughts that keep you from looking forward.

Your mind and heart have many wonderful things to dwell on each day. Give thanks to God for placing a rainbow of promise in your path.

Dear God: Thank you for the wonderful and creative work you are doing in my life. Help me look forward to each new day. Amen.

Forget the former things; do not dwell on the past. See, I am doing a new thing!

Isaiah 43:18–19 NIV

LOOKING UP TO YOU

I am an example to many people, because you are my strong protection.

Psalm 71:7 NCV

arents often laugh about the way their small children pick up phrases they hear around the house—which are often repeated at inopportune times. Yet children are innocent and just want to be like their mom or dad.

You, on the other hand, are not a child any longer, but still pick up habits—good and bad—from friends, co-workers, and others.

However, God has commanded that you set his Word as your standard for living, obeying anything he commands you to do.

Friend, just as the Lord expects you to set a godly pattern for your loved ones, he also wants you to follow his holy example. Therefore, look to him and imitate his honorable character—because surely his ways will protect you forever.

You will make me truly great and take my sorrow away.

Psalm 71:21 CEV

God, forgive me for the times I have compromised my testimony of your love. I know what is right, and I ask that you help me to live in step with your truth. Amen.

MAKING OF A SAINT

Train yourself in godliness.
1 Timothy 4:7 NRSV

While holiness sounds like an ethereal concept reserved for the rarefied air of a convent, it's actually a down-to-earth, observable, and practicable lifestyle. It's the lifestyle God has in mind for you.

God educates you in the ways of holiness as you read the Bible and allow his Spirit to enter those places in your heart and life needing light and warmth. He helps you use the experiences and conditions that you encounter daily to bring you toward a more complete and thorough holiness and godly stature.

If you haven't already guessed, God is preparing you for sainthood, because in Jesus you're a saint in his eyes right now.

Pursue a righteous life—a life of wonder, faith, love, steadiness, courtesy.

1 Timothy 6:11 THE MESSAGE

Heavenly Father: You have put before me all I need to live the life of a saint. Train me in your ways and help me become a true example of godliness to others. Amen.

BE CAREFUL
WHOM YOU FOLLOW

Give the gift of wise rule to the king, O God. . . . May he judge your
people rightly, be honorable to your meek and lowly.

Psalm 72:1–2 THE MESSAGE

Every day you receive many messages—people expressing
their opinions on the television, radio, and in conversation.
Many have strong views and make viable cases for why you should
have the same outlook as theirs. God cautions you to be wise and
not believe all you hear.

God is straightforward in his approach to right and wrong—and
you can be sure that anything that contradicts his Word is false
and destructive. So do not get caught in the trap of thinking
he does not really care what you do. He will not ignore your
unfaithfulness.

Lord God, you are truly
a worthy leader, and I
love your ways. Please
help me to embrace
your truth and to apply
it correctly to my life.
Amen.

The Lord has only the best in mind for
your life, and he is motivated to see you
enjoy it. However, it all begins with your
obedience to him. Therefore, do as he
says, because he really is worth following.

Praise be to the Lord God, the God of Israel,
who alone does marvelous deeds. Praise be
to his glorious name forever; may the whole
earth be filled with his glory.

Psalm 72:18–19 NIV

HIS RIGHTFUL PLACE

God is the king of the whole earth. Make your best music for him!

Psalm 47:7 GOD'S WORD

When visiting heads of state, it is customary to bring a gift. Certainly no mediocre offering will do. You must present the dignitary with a meaningful item that represents your respect for them.

Unfortunately, most people do not approach God with the same reverence. Whereas people will offer their best to earthly leaders, they believe their Creator will be satisfied with the leftovers. They give him a few seconds of prayer, a minute or two of Bible reading, and an honorable mention now and again, and they think it is enough.

God, please forgive my not honoring you as I should. Help me to give you my very best today and every day — just as you deserve. Amen.

Yet understand, there is no higher sovereign than God. When all other rulers have turned to dust, he remains Lord of all that exists. He deserves your absolute best. So stop presenting him with halfhearted offerings. Give God his rightful place in your life and truly honor him.

Clap your hands, all you peoples! Shout to God with the voice of triumph! For the Lord Most High is awesome; He is a great King over all the earth.

Psalm 47:1–2 NKJV

AT HIS WORD

I will come and proclaim your mighty acts, O Sovereign Lord; I will proclaim your righteousness, yours alone.

Psalm 71:16 NIV

Would anyone serve a god who is weak and easily manipulated, one without authority? You would not be serving a god at all. The God of the Bible is sovereign, the holder of ultimate authority. At his word, the heavens came into being. At his word, *you* came into being. He is the author, the initiator, the creator of the woman you are.

Dear God: Thank you for loving me just as I am. May I walk in humble submission to your power and will. Amen.

Does it surprise you to learn that God knows you so well and still loves you so much? He does! He can't be talked into changing his mind. He simply chooses to love you, and by his mighty Word, he promises that fact will never change.

I look to you for help, O Sovereign Lord. You are my refuge.

Psalm 141:8 NLT

September 14

LIFELONG LEARNING

Let us leave the elementary teachings about Christ and go on to maturity.

Hebrews 6:1 NIV

Many women consider themselves lifelong learners. No matter how many years they have been out of school, these women eagerly examine new subjects and readily welcome new knowledge and discoveries.

In calling you to faith, God has put you on a path of lifelong learning. After you accept his plan of salvation, God invites you to explore his many mysteries and delve more deeply into his treasury of biblical wisdom. He encourages you to let your questions take you even further into his Word, because in finding answers you grow in faith.

Dear God: I want to continue to learn about you and the truths you have put before me. I desire to become a knowledgeable and mature Christian. Amen.

Spend your lifetime having the time of your life learning about him.

Teach the righteous and they will gain in learning.

Proverbs 9:9 NRSV

YOUR TEACHER AND COUNSELOR

Teach me to do your will, for you are my God. May your gracious Spirit lead me forward on a firm footing.

Psalm 143:10 NLT

*S*ometimes following God seems more confusing than it really is. You want to be faithful to him, but other than obeying a list of rules, you are not sure how. Isn't being a Christian more than just abiding by biblical regulations?

Of course it is! Believing in God means enjoying a wonderful relationship with him based on love. So how do you learn to please him?

God, thank you for teaching me how to love and serve you! Even in this, you are guiding me faithfully. Truly you are worthy of all honor, glory, and praise! Amen.

Always remember that the God who is able to save you from your sins is able to teach you to live a life of love and faithfulness to him. He will patiently instruct you in how to follow him and do his will. So trust and obey him, because the Christian life is truly the most wonderful worth living.

Teach me the way in which I should walk; for to You I lift up my soul.

Psalm 143:8 NASB

DRAWING STRENGTH FROM STILLNESS

Cease striving and know that I am God; I will be exalted among the nations, I will be exalted in the earth.

Psalm 46:10 NASB

The swift pace and challenges of life can leave you weary and disheartened if you never take time to rest in your relationship with God. That is why it is crucial for you to be quiet before him, surrendering yourself and your struggles to him as an offering.

Be silent and relax, confident that he can handle everything that concerns you. Meditate on his sufficiency. Surely nothing is impossible for Almighty God—the glorious Creator of heaven and earth. Enjoy his presence and allow his Spirit to encourage your heart. Receive his mighty strength and wonderful wisdom for every burden you carry.

It is in the stillness that God will give you the confidence and endurance for everything that comes your way. So know him, friend, and find peace.

God, I sit before you in quiet expectation. Please help me to be calm and focus on you. Fill me with your peace and strength, and I will praise your name. Amen.

Come, behold the works of the Lord.

Psalm 46:8 NKJV

THE GOD YOU LOVE

Who is this great king? He is the Lord, strong and mighty, the Lord, victorious in battle.

Psalm 24:8 GNT

o you love God for what he does or because of who he is? Do you pay him lip service to get what you want, or do you worship him because you are truly in awe of his amazing grace?

Like you, God desires to be loved for himself—for you to honor him because he is astoundingly imaginative, unwaveringly kind, steadfastly holy, completely powerful, and absolutely wise. He also wants to have a deep, abiding relationship with you so you can experience his unconditional love.

So consider: Why do you seek him? Are you looking for someone to cater to your needs? Or have you realized that you are simply not whole without him in your life? Do you praise him for your sake or for his?

God, I want to love you for who you are—even though my motivation is sometimes misplaced. Help me to know you and love you more every day. Amen.

The earth is the Lord's, and all it contains, the world, and those who dwell in it.

Psalm 24:1 NASB

GOOD EVIDENCE

The heavens keep telling the wonders of God, and the skies declare what he has done.

Psalm 19:1 CEV

As you stand in awe of a sunset or are enthralled by a rainbow, you may find yourself contemplating God's magnificent handiwork. Clearly, the beauty, brilliance, and mystery of the universe attest to God's presence and his power.

Because God has sent his Spirit to work in you, your life also offers evidence of God's presence and power. When you know God, and you conform your thoughts, words, and actions to his will, your very being announces his living and personal goodness. Those who look at you cannot help but see what his Spirit has done. His glory shines brightly in you. God's strength becomes your strength.

Dear God: Grant me a heart of praise for the wonders of your creation and gratitude for the goodness you have worked in me. Amen.

We rejoice in the hope of the glory of God.

Romans 5:2 NIV

TREASURES OF THE HEART

In everything you do, put God first, and he will direct you and crown your efforts with success.

Proverbs 3:6 TLB

The woman placed her grandmother's porcelain tray in her china cabinet alongside a glass figurine she'd bought on a trip to Asia. She protects these treasures because they are precious to her, and she enjoys looking at them.

The forefront of your heart is like a spiritual china cabinet where you place your most cherished hopes, dreams, memories, and desires. You look at them often, and you take hold of every opportunity to bring them into your life.

God sees the things you cherish, and he knows their intrinsic quality and eternal value. He invites you to talk with him about the treasures he prizes above all else.

Heavenly Father: Look into my heart and help me choose to cherish those things you care about and those things you hold above all others. Amen.

Take delight in the Lord, and he will give you the desires of your heart.

Psalm 37:4 NRSV

DEDICATED AND OBEDIENT

Oh, that my actions would consistently reflect your principles!

Psalm 119:5 NLT

The psalmist discovered the blessing of agreeing with God. To follow his instructions is to experience liberty and joy beyond what the heart can ever know on its own.

As orator and clergyman Henry Ward Beecher wrote, "The strength and happiness of a man consists in finding out the way in which God is going, and going in that way too."

Not that it is ever easy—by any means. You will find it is challenging to practice his principles. However, if you are dedicated and obey him out of love, you will find that the way he is going leads to the destination you've always longed to reach.

> Be good to me, your servant, so that I may live and obey your teachings. Open my eyes, so that I may see the wonderful truths in your law.
>
> Psalm 119:17–18 GNT

God, please help me to be dedicated and obedient to your principles so that I can learn your wonderful truth and follow wherever you go. Amen.

THE RIGHT STEP

Wisdom begins with respect for the Lord; those who obey his orders have good understanding. He should be praised forever.

Psalm 111:10 NCV

*H*ave you ever longed to know what was going to happen in the future? You may be facing a problematic situation and want to make the best choice in the matter. Or perhaps you have been given an exciting opportunity and question whether moving forward is the right thing to do.

God's will is not a mystery. He has a wonderful path that he wants you to follow, but you must be willing to do two things: First, ask him to reveal his plan to you. Second, be committed to obeying him even if it means making a difficult decision.

You may be tempted to move forward without him, but don't. Wait until you know his will, because he will certainly show you the right step to take.

Thank you, God, for revealing your will to me when I fully place my trust in you. You are faithful and true, and worthy of all praise. Amen.

All he does is just and good, and all his commandments are trustworthy. They are forever true, to be obeyed faithfully and with integrity.

Psalm 111:7–8 NLT

THE SEEDS OF WONDERS

He said to me, "My grace is sufficient for you, for My strength is made perfect in weakness."

2 Corinthians 12:9 NKJV

A woman, excited about her new property, planted a big garden. Though books advise novices to start small, and friends questioned the size of her project, she enthusiastically forged ahead with her plans. Soon the care and maintenance of her lot overwhelmed her. She admitted, "I've learned a lesson—the hard way."

If you have learned a lesson through an unfortunate experience, give thanks, because you are on the road to spiritual maturity and wisdom. You have discovered the value of good counsel and the merit of careful judgment. This is knowledge you can take and use in every future endeavor.

Dear God: Thank you for supporting me and strengthening me so I can become the woman you have created me to be. Amen.

In the seeds of frailty, God plants mighty wonders.

We know that in all things God works for the good of those who love him, who have been called according to his purpose.

Romans 8:28 NIV

USELESS IDOLS

Our Lord is greater than all gods. . . . The idols of the nations are of silver and gold, made by human hands. They have mouths, but cannot speak, eyes, but cannot see.

Psalm 135:5, 15–16 HCSB

Anything can become an idol in your life—relationships, activities, food, work, money, shopping, drugs—*anything*. You know it's taken over your heart because you'd forsake God for the pleasure and false security it offers. Sadly, it always leaves you wanting more—you're unfulfilled, isolated, and it's slowly destroying your life.

Do you find yourself heartbroken and unsatisfied more often than not? Is there an emptiness in you that nothing can fill? Your idol cannot help you—it knows nothing of your needs. It can only take, not give.

God sees your needs and supplies them. He hears your heart and provides you with understanding in a way that nothing else can.

God, please forgive me for seeking useless idols. Truly only you can satisfy my soul in a way that gives me life and joy. I choose you, God, and I praise you! Amen.

When you feel empty, turn to him and have confidence that he will help you. He will surely fill you to overflowing.

Everyone who makes idols and all who trust them will end up as helpless as their idols.

Psalm 135:18 CEV

SOMEONE WORTH KNOWING

Skilled living gets its start in the Fear-of-God, insight into life from knowing a Holy God.

Proverbs 9:10 THE MESSAGE

Imagine that you've made a new friend. You want to learn all about the new person in your life. You can't wait for conversations to begin.

God is also a friend worth knowing. Unlike the wooden statues some worship, he is accessible. He wants to be known. He's told you all about himself in his Word, and he waits enthusiastically for the dialogue to begin.

If your heart longs to know him, to grasp who he really is and what he wants from you, sit down with an open heart and an open Bible and get to know the God of the universe, who loves you with an everlasting love.

Wonderful Father: Thank you for reaching out to me and opening the door to a loving, everlasting relationship between the two of us. Thank you for allowing me to know you. Amen.

Thanks be to God, who in Christ always leads us in triumphal procession, and through us spreads in every place the fragrance that comes from knowing him.

2 Corinthians 2:14 NRSV

WHAT DO I DO?

Make Your ways known to me, Lord; teach me Your paths. Guide me in Your truth and teach me, for You are the God of my salvation; I wait for You all day long.

Psalm 25:4–5 HCSB

"I don't know what to do." This is difficult to admit if you are accustomed to being self-sufficient and finding your own way in every situation. When this realization settles in, the anxiety may overwhelm you, especially if others are depending upon you to do what is best. With all options exhausted, where can you turn?

God, it is so hard to give up control. Please forgive me for being so resistant to your direction. Thank you for your gentleness and for helping me through this trial. Amen.

These circumstances did not happen by chance. God will allow you to reach the end of your resources so you will turn to him and seek his guidance.

Friend, stop being so self-reliant. Instead of trying to figure out what to do or thinking that you must have all the answers, pray to him. Read the Bible. Listen for his direction. He *does* know what to do, and he will certainly show you the very best path to take.

Those who respect the Lord? He will point them to the best way. . . . My eyes are always looking to the Lord for help. He will keep me from any traps.

Psalm 25:12, 15 NCV

WORDS OF LOVE

Christ's love . . . has the first and last word in everything we do.

2 Corinthians 5:14 THE MESSAGE

God wants you to have the first word—and the last word too.

When you approach your day with an attitude of loving-kindness toward the people you meet and the tasks you perform, every word you speak refreshes and renews those relationships like a gentle spring rain. Your speech plants the seeds of kindness, and your actions cultivate harmony and understanding between people. When you close your day with the same mindset, the last things you say leave behind God's blessing and the sweet fragrance of his peace.

Dear God: In my walk with you, help me learn the great power of your love at work through me in everything I say and do today. Amen.

When you walk in relationship with God, love is the first word and the last word, and they both belong to you.

Pleasing words are like honey. They are sweet to the soul and healing to the bones.

Proverbs 16:24 NLV

SPA TIME

Those who let distress drive them away from God are full of regrets.

2 Corinthians 7:10 THE MESSAGE

For many, there's nothing more soothing than soaking in a deep, warm bubble bath. Minor aches and pains seem to drift away, you are refreshed and rejuvenated, and the moments of quiet ease the mind as well.

God's forgiveness is like a cleansing, reenergizing bath for the spirit. Immerse yourself in him; he washes your guilt away with his all-encompassing comfort and the assurance of his love. You are given the healing balm of complete pardon, and you emerge ready and able to follow him more closely and listen to him more attentively.

God's way changes you, and always for the better.

Dear God: Thank you for replacing my sadness and guilt with joy and thanksgiving. Bathe me in the refreshing waters of your peace. Amen.

Let us draw near to God with a sincere heart in full assurance of faith, having our hearts sprinkled to cleanse us from a guilty conscience and having our bodies washed with pure water.

Hebrews 10:22 NIV

LISTEN EXPECTANTLY

God spoke in holy splendor.
Psalm 108:7 THE MESSAGE

Have you ever prayed for God to meet a need in a certain way but the answer did not come immediately? You continued to seek his will but it appeared that he was silent about the matter.

God is always at work. However, you may not see the many ways he is orchestrating the blessings he sends. How should you wait for your prayers to be answered? One of the best ways is to wait with confident expectation, knowing that he is the God of the universe and that he is intimately involved in your life.

God, I proclaim my faith in you. You set the heavens and the earth in place, and I know you will meet every need I have with your great power and wisdom. Amen.

Never be quick to jump ahead of him. Waiting with patience and with hopeful expectation of his provision is a demonstration of your faith in his ability to meet every need you have.

With God we will gain the victory.
Psalm 108:13 NIV

297

Soul-Deep Joy

The joy of the Lord is your strength!
Nehemiah 8:10 NLT

hemotherapy had taken its toll on her hair, weight, and energy, yet her friends could not help but notice the aura of transcendent joy emanating from deep within one remarkable woman. The reason was her trust in God.

The joy of the Lord, understandable when times are good, startles when its presence persists, even increases, when the days turn difficult. This is the kind of joy God has for you, a joy you hold on to that astonishes people as it continues to deepen and strengthen despite hardships and regardless of adverse circumstances.

Nothing has the power to steal from you the soul-deep joy that is yours in God.

Heavenly Father:
In all things, let me
rejoice in your great
love and put my trust
in you, and let my
happiness find its
home in you alone.
Amen.

You will live in joy and peace. The mountains and hills, the trees of the field—all the world around you—will rejoice.

Isaiah 55:12 TLB

ASSURED IN HIS PRESENCE

God is within her, she will not fall; God will help her at break of day.

Psalm 46:5 NIV

Assyrian soldiers were known for their ruthless obliteration of any nation that dared resist their progress. When the invading army drew near to Jerusalem, King Hezekiah had a tough choice to make. Should he surrender unconditionally to the Assyrians in the hope of saving his people? Or should he trust God to deliver them?

In a leap of faith, Hezekiah chose the Lord. Psalm 46 is thought by some to be the song of triumph written when God honored Hezekiah's faithfulness and delivered Jerusalem.

Has God been leading you to make a very difficult decision? Like Jerusalem, you will not fall as long as you trust in God and obey him. So take the leap of faith and be confident that he will lead you victoriously.

> God is our Refuge and Strength [mighty and impenetrable to temptation], a very present and well-proved help in trouble.
>
> Psalm 46:1 AMP

O God, you know the struggle I am having with this decision. Yet I will have faith and do as you say. Please protect me, and lead me to victory. Amen.

OCTOBER

The Lord God gives me the
right words to encourage the weary.
Each morning he awakens me
eager to learn his teaching.

ISAIAH 50:4 CEV

STABILITY

Now I stand on solid ground, and I will publicly praise the Lord.

Psalm 26:12 NLT

Where do you go for stability? When your world crumbles around you, where do you turn? Friend, God should not be your last resort.

Because when chaotic situations occur, only he can steady you with his assurance, teach you wisdom and self-control, and train you to remain faithful. Rather than allowing events to throw you off balance, he shows you how to stay in the center of his will and cling to his unwavering promises.

God is the only One who can truly bring you stability because he is completely consistent and unchanging—he stays steady, though the rest of the world may tremble. Therefore, stand on solid ground by setting your feet on the path God has for you. There, you will surely never be shaken.

God, what would I do without you to cling to? I praise you for your faultless character that I can always depend upon. Truly you are wonderful. Amen.

Your steadfast love is before my eyes, and I walk in your faithfulness.

Psalm 26:3 ESV

October 2

FAMILY TIES

A wise woman strengthens her family.

Proverbs 14:1 NCV

At some point in life, many women find themselves in the role of sole or contributing caregiver for children, parents, or other relatives.

When you respond willingly and wholeheartedly to the needs of your family members, you are following God's plan for families—that is, a group of people devoted to helping, encouraging, and nurturing one another, and who create a safe, comfortable, and nurturing environment for everyone.

Your status as daughter, wife, mother, aunt, or grandmother offers you the privilege and opportunity to strengthen the bonds between the people in your family. Your relationship with God inspires you to do so with joy and gladness.

Dear God: Grant me a generous heart and willing hands to care for the members of my family. Help me find ways to enrich and strengthen our bonds. Amen.

It takes wisdom to have a good family, and it takes understanding to make it strong.

Proverbs 24:3 NCV

October 3

RECEIVING YOUR PRAYERS

Go in peace. And may the God of Israel give you what you have asked of him.

1 Samuel 1:17 THE MESSAGE

More than anything else in the world, Hannah wanted a baby. She often wept while she prayed because her desire for a child was so ingrained and impassioned.

Is there something that you desire with that intensity? What is it that brings tears to your eyes when you think about it for too long?

Let peace permeate your soul—God has received your prayers. If he has promised to fulfill your deepest longing, you can count on the fact that he will. He gave Hannah her child, and he will grant your request as well.

Take heart that God receives your prayers. Wipe away your tears and receive his peace.

God, thank you so much for receiving my prayers and for drying my tears. I will wait for your answer and fully embrace your peace. Amen.

The Lord gave me what I asked Him.

1 Samuel 1:27 HCSB

HE CALLS YOU BEAUTIFUL

The king is enthralled by your beauty; honor him, for he is your lord.

Psalm 45:11 NIV

Today before you look in the mirror and pick yourself apart, think about this wonderful truth: God finds you lovely. He created every detail that makes you unique—your personality, giftedness, and traits—with loving care, and he is enthralled with what he has accomplished.

You are precious to God. Filled with potential, every facet of who you are is beautiful to him. Yet what he loves most about you is that your heart, which has been cleansed with his forgiveness and covered with his righteousness, now longs to know, honor, and obey him.

So as you look in the mirror, praise him for how he made you, even those things you wish you could change. Then gaze into his face and realize that your beauty is really a reflection of his.

God, how wonderful it is to be loved so deeply and completely. Fill my eyes with your magnificent face, and my heart with your wonderful love. Amen.

You love righteousness and hate wickedness; therefore God, your God, has set you above your companions by anointing you with the oil of joy.

Psalm 45:7 NIV

HUMAN NATURE

*Their hearts were not really loyal to God. . . . Still God was merciful.
. . . He remembered that they were only human, like a wind that blows
and does not come back.*

Psalm 78:37–39 NCV

Even when you are unfaithful, God never stops loving you. He loves you with an enduring love that is both infinite and unconditional. You cannot do anything to derail his love for you.

Sin harms your fellowship with him because it produces feelings of guilt and shame and causes you to wonder if he still cares for you. Yet understand, although he will not approve of sin, he will never withhold his love from you—he still offers it freely.

So how do you handle the times when your human nature tempts you to yield to sin? The best course of action is to ask God to teach you more about his love. Because when you understand how great his love for you is, you will never want to drift in your devotion to him.

*God, I want to honor
you. Thank you for
not holding my past
against me. Thank
you for forgiving me,
loving me, and making
me new. Amen.*

[God] led His own people forth like sheep and guided them [with a shepherd's care] like a flock in the wilderness. And He led them on safely and in confident trust, so that they feared not.

Psalm 78:52–53 AMP

LOVE AND CREATION

The God whose skill formed the cosmos, His love never quits.
The God who laid out earth on ocean foundations, His love
never quits.

Psalm 136:5–6 THE MESSAGE

Have you ever considered that the creation didn't have to be so spectacular? It wasn't necessary for there to be a full spectrum of fragrant flowers for you to admire or colorful birds to entertain you with their lovely songs. The mountains with their rugged heights, the valleys with their verdant panoramas, the briny beauty of the oceans—none of these landscapes had to exist. But they do.

> *God, thank you for such an amazing world and for loving me so much! Help me to know your love and show you love in return. Amen.*

Why? God created everything for you to enjoy. In this way, he reveals himself to you and expresses his love for you.

God always goes the extra mile to show you his love—and the creation is full evidence of this fact. So don't doubt him, friend. Surely he will always provide for your needs and satisfy your soul in a manner beyond all you could ask or imagine.

> Give thanks to the Lord of lords, for his steadfast love endures forever; to him who alone does great wonders, for his steadfast love endures forever.
>
> Psalm 136:3–4 ESV

October 7

WOUNDS FROM A FRIEND

In return for my love, they accuse me, but I pray for them.
Psalm 109:4 GOD'S WORD

Have you ever experienced the betrayal of a friend? What should you do when such an awful thing happens? The psalmist turned his attention to God. He did not run to others declaring his side of the story, trying to gain support. Instead, he sought shelter in God's presence.

God is the only One who can offer the proper view of your circumstances. He helps you recall the many times you have fallen short in the same way and prepares you to forgive the person who hurt you.

Why? Because anger and resentment are unbearable weights that restrict your ability to experience his love. You can forgive those who hurt you and move on when the focus of your heart is set on the Savior.

God, please teach me how to extend grace and mercy to those who have hurt me. Root out any bitterness, God, and heal my wounds. Amen.

Lord, deal kindly with me for Your name's sake; because Your lovingkindness is good, deliver me; for I am afflicted and needy, and my heart is wounded within me.

Psalm 109:21–22 NASB

FREE FOR THE TAKING

How rich is God's grace, which he has given to us so fully and freely.

Ephesians 1:7–8 NCV

Whether you were born to shop or are someone who goes shopping only out of necessity, you know you never get something of value for nothing. If someone offers you an expensive item at no cost, you have every reason to start asking questions.

The rules of the earthly marketplace don't apply in heaven. God's compassion comes to you completely free. You need only accept it. He guarantees you his mercy and kindness now and throughout eternity. It's simply God's good pleasure to show such love to you.

> *Dear God: I give thanks for the mercy, compassion, and kindness you show toward me. You have been gracious to me. Amen.*

Put away your wallet and open yourself to the wonder of God's grace. It's yours for the taking.

From his abundance we have all received one gracious blessing after another.

John 1:16 NLT

October 9

October 9

IT ISN'T FAIR!

I had nearly lost confidence; my faith was almost gone because I was jealous of the proud when I saw that things go well for the wicked.

Psalm 73:2–3 GNT

There are times when life seems unjust, and you will have to find a way to deal with what you have experienced. People can do and say things that are reckless and cruel. However, whenever you feel ignored or rejected, you have an important choice to make: Either you can become bitter or you can become better. You can stew in your anger or move on with the knowledge of God's personal love for you.

God, thank you for understanding my hurts and my feelings. Help me to do the same for others when they act without reason or care. Amen.

God's priceless comfort can soften the impact of others' thoughtless words and deeds. So keep your eyes on him. Listen for his voice of encouragement and be willing to forgive those who have hurt you. This is what Jesus did—he forgave because he knew those who accused him did not know the truth.

In heaven I have only you, and on this earth you are all I want. My body and mind may fail, but you are my strength and my choice forever.

Psalm 73:25–26 CEV

October 10

DIVINE POSSIBILITIES

Humanly speaking, it is impossible. But with God everything is possible.

Matthew 19:26 NLT

God does not ask you to do things that are humanly possible. He does not fill your heart with goals that you could easily achieve on your own.

Rather, God gives you dreams that are far bigger and more wonderful than you could ever aspire to, dreams that can only be accomplished if he is actively involved in your life.

Why? Because God wants you to know that the good that happens to you is from him—so that you will seek, experience, and rely upon him.

He is bringing the hopes that burn in you into being. So trust him to make all those impossible dreams come true.

Lord All-Powerful, you are God. You have promised me some very good things, and you can be trusted to do what you promise.

2 Samuel 7:28 CEV

God, with you are divine possibilities. Thank you for letting me join your spectacular plans, and for teaching me to love you more in the process. Amen.

October 11

ALL YOU REALLY NEED

Not in my bow do I trust, nor can my sword save me. But you have saved us. . . . In God we have boasted continually, and we will give thanks to your name forever.

Psalm 44:6–8 ESV

*K*ing Jehoshaphat of Judah realized that his nation did not stand a chance against the invading armies of Ammon, Moab, and Mount Seir. So he prayed, asking the Lord for instruction. God's direction to him went against all conventional wisdom. Instead of fighting the enemy with swords and bows, the people of Judah were to worship the Lord with singing. So they did. They praised him as their enemies advanced. And miraculously, he won their battle for them.

God, I have been fretting because I do not have the resources for the challenge I face today. Thank you for showing me that all I need is to obey you. Amen.

Are you facing a challenge that seems overwhelming to you today? Seek God's guidance. His instructions may not make sense, but obey him anyway, doing exactly as he says. He will surely triumph in this battle for you, and he will teach you that he is all you really need.

It wasn't their power that gave them victory. But it was your great power and strength. You were with them because you loved them.

Psalm 44:3 NCV

HE CARES FOR YOU

Keep yourself pure.
1 Timothy 5:22 NIV

ou have full permission to take care of yourself, not only from health counselors, but from God.

The Bible says God created your body and gave you life, complete with intelligence, feelings, emotions, soul, and spirit. He wants you to care for your whole person, and he offers many ways for you to do that.

You care for yourself his way when you avoid unhealthy habits of body and mind and keep yourself as physically, mentally, and spiritually fit as possible. Yes, taking care of yourself takes time and effort, but God is pleased when you make it a priority. He wants you to be always at the "top of your game."

Creator-God:
Thank you for your
eternal loving care
for me. Grant me a
heart ready to do those
things I need to do
for my own physical,
emotional, and
spiritual well-being.
Amen.

I shall yet praise him, who is the health of my countenance, and my God.
Psalm 43:5 KJV

HOW TO BE BEAUTIFUL

Those who walk uprightly enter into peace.
Isaiah 57:2 NIV

*G*enuine beauty grows from a peaceful soul. Inner harmony leaves a woman's face free of tension, and her mind and heart free to love and care for others.

As you continue to obey God's commandments and discover his will, you will notice a difference in how you feel and how you look. Your peace, a peace possible only from a clear conscience and a reliance on God's power in your life, transforms you. You feel in harmony with yourself, and you find your tranquility reflected in the mirror.

Your friends may remark on your sparkling eyes or your welcoming smile, but what they're really seeing is your beautiful soul.

The fruit of righteousness will be peace; the effect of righteousness will be quietness and confidence forever.

Isaiah 32:17 NIV

Dear God: I yearn for the beauty possessed by women at peace with themselves and secure in their relationship with you. Give me a soul immersed in you! Amen.

WHATEVER HE WANTS

*Even if it isn't what we want to do. We will obey the Lord so
that all will go well for us.*

Jeremiah 42:6 CEV

*Y*ou never go wrong when you commit your way to
God. He is always faithful to lead you in the very
best way. And he promises that if you obey him he will protect
you and cause you to prosper.

Sometimes his instructions will seem counterintuitive—very
different from what you expected. And it will take real courage and faith to obey him because his instructions will not make sense from your
standpoint. However, you can always be
confident that God has excellent reasons
for his commands—reasons of your protection and your prosperity.

Take heart and commit to being faithful and obeying God today. Assuredly,
you'll be glad that you did.

*God, sometimes it is
hard to obey, but I
trust you to lead me
well. Thank you that
all of your commands
are good. Amen.*

Listen to and obey My voice, and I will be your God and you will be My
people; and walk in the whole way that I command you, that it may be
well with you.

Jeremiah 7:23 AMP

Keep in mind always
that the ultimate Master you're
serving is Christ.

COLOSSIANS 3:24 THE MESSAGE

NEVER DESPAIR

I would have despaired unless I had believed that I would see the goodness of the Lord in the land of the living.

Psalm 27:13 NASB

D espair can drive you to all sorts of destructive behaviors. You become so anxious to see your desires fulfilled that you turn to options that oppose God's best for you. You may even convince yourself that he has abandoned you.

Of course, that is untrue. God *will* help you, in his timing. Yet that is why you need to protect yourself from despair while you are waiting for him to work—so you do not miss his perfect will for you.

Therefore, meditate daily on his Word, on his promises, and on the occasions he has rescued you, because then it is so much easier to hold on to your hope. Wait expectantly for God's goodness no matter how long it takes, because that is the perfect position to be in to receive his very best.

God, thank you for rescuing me when I have come so close to despair. Help me to stay steadfast in hope and to always trust your perfect will. Amen.

Wait on the Lord; be of good courage, and He shall strengthen your heart; wait, I say, on the Lord!

Psalm 27:14 NKJV

JOY TODAY

The Spirit of God has made me; the breath of the Almighty gives me life.

Job 33:4 NIV

omeone once said, "To dream of the woman you would like to be in the future is to waste the woman you are right now."

The woman you are right now is a woman beloved of God, a woman he welcomes with tender love and deep compassion. He knows your heart, your thoughts, and your feelings with an intimacy beyond anyone's knowledge of you, even beyond the knowledge you have of yourself. He shares this with you so you can enjoy yourself and take pleasure in the life you live and each day he has given to you.

> *Almighty God: Surround me with your life-giving presence, enabling me to grasp the wonder of my life and delight in the woman I am today. Amen.*

There's happiness in being you, because Almighty God has made you who you are.

With you [O Lord] is the fountain of life; in your light we see light.

Psalm 36:9 NIV

BOUNTIFUL AND BEAUTIFUL

[Jesus said:] "The thief comes only to steal and kill and destroy; I came that they may have life, and have it abundantly."

John 10:10 NASB

Think of the woman you most admire. Chances are she inspires you to strive for excellence and motivates you to make changes for the better in your life. Simply put, her example leads you to enrich your life.

In the same way, God wants to enrich your life with his many and plentiful blessings. When you look up to him, you see the beauty and peace he offers, and you begin to bring those things into your life. As you read the Bible, you learn more about God, and you find yourself making choices and decisions based on his will.

For a bountiful and beautiful life, look up to him.

Return, O my soul, to your rest, for the Lord has dealt bountifully with you.

Psalm 116:7 NRSV

Dear God: Thank you for showing me how full, rich, and abundant life can be. I cherish the blessings you show me each day. Amen.

PROVISION FROM HEAVEN

He brought quail and satisfied them with bread from heaven. He opened a rock, and water gushed out; it flowed like a stream in the desert. For He remembered His holy promise.

Psalm 105:40–42 HCSB

Many people are tangled up in their thoughts because they have forgotten what God has promised them in the Bible. You do not have to follow the same path. God wants you to understand that his mercies are new every morning and that he will provide for you in miraculous ways as you travel through life.

One way he does so is through the Bible, which contains all the hope and wisdom you need for each day. Do not think that the Bible was written for someone else who lived in another place and time. That isn't true. The Bible was written for you, and the truth it contains is just as powerful today as when it was first penned. When God promises to love, provide for, and guide you each day, he means it.

> *Thank you, God, that your mercies are new every morning and your care for me never changes. Teach me through the Bible how to walk in your way. Amen.*

> He brought Israel out with silver and gold, and no one among his tribes stumbled. . . . He spread out a cloud as a protective covering and a fire to light up the night.

Psalm 105:37, 39 GOD'S WORD

October 19

IN HIS PRESENCE

I am continually with you; you hold my right hand.

Psalm 73:23 NRSV

You can feel lonely in a room by yourself, and you can feel lonely in a crowd. You may not understand why you are overcome with the sense of distance and separation that can make you feel small and weak. Whatever the cause, God offers a guaranteed solution.

Meditate on God's love for you, a love beyond all human understanding. Because he values you so much, he has promised to never let you move out of his embrace or away from his hand of goodness. By yourself or in a crowd, you can rely on God, who is always by your side. With God, you are never alone.

God in heaven: I give thanks to you for the security of knowing you are with me wherever I go. I am never alone. Amen.

"[God is] right there with you. He won't let you down; he won't leave you."

Deuteronomy 31:6 THE MESSAGE

October 20

THE GREAT ARCHITECT

The day is Yours, also the night; You established the moon and the sun. You set all the boundaries of the earth.

Psalm 74:16–17 HCSB

With the changing political climate of our world, it would be easy to wonder if God is in control. The answer is yes. The One who established the boundaries for the land and sea, and set the moon and stars in their places, watches over you.

God, I want a glimpse of your greatness. Whether changes occur in my life or on the world stage, I will watch for your sovereign hand and trust you always. Amen.

When life appears to be spiraling out of control, you can be assured that God is not affected. Sudden changes do not surprise or move him—he remains the same yesterday, today, and forever.

When problems come, your first reaction may be one of anxiety. But God is sovereign, and he challenges you to recall the times he has kept you safe, protected your heart, and provided for every need you have. Always remember, nothing is too difficult for him to handle. No, friend—nothing at all.

God my king is from ancient times, performing saving acts on the earth.

Psalm 74:12 HCSB

LEARNING TO LOVE HIM

I will go to the altar of God, to God my exceeding joy; and upon the lyre I shall praise You, O God, my God.

Psalm 43:4 NASB

he student who studies to play an instrument with a mediocre teacher will take on the shortcomings of her mentor. It is only through the patient training of a skilled maestro that she is able to unlearn any faulty technique and discover the true art of her instrument.

The same is true for love. Sometimes people are negatively influenced by those who first love them, and their devotion to God falls short. The wonderful thing about God is that he gladly teaches people how to love him.

Did you have a flawed example of love when you were growing up? Do not despair. The great Maestro will show you the most excellent way to express love and be loved in return. So learn from him, friend, and sing his praises with joy.

God, you are the great Maestro of my heart. Teach me to love as you do, unconditionally, sacrificially, with joy and trust. To you be all the glory. Amen.

Send your light and your truth. Let them guide me. Let them bring me to your holy mountain and to your dwelling place.

Psalm 43:3 GOD'S WORD

OUT OF THE BLUE

We'll never comprehend all the great things he does; his miracle-surprises can't be counted.

Job 9:10 THE MESSAGE

*Y*ou've heard the expression "Life is full of surprises," and you probably can think of several examples from your own experience. When you couldn't see a solution to a problem, one popped up seemingly out of nowhere.

God moves events to work for your good, even when you don't understand why something is happening to you. He cares about your plans for the day, week, and year, but he sees your plans in light of all eternity, and he may choose to provide for you in a way you could not have anticipated.

When you walk with God, expect the unexpected. He has great and joyful things waiting for you.

May the Lord direct your hearts to the love of God and to the steadfastness of Christ.

2 Thessalonians 3:5 NRSV

Dear God: In difficult days when I have no answers, grant me patience as I await the joyful news you have in store for me. Amen.

PLANNED KINDNESS

Do what is right and true. Be kind and merciful to each other.

Zechariah 7:9 NCV

Practice random acts of kindness," a catch-phrase of the mid-1990s, describes a good deed done for a stranger with no thought of receiving anything in return. God goes beyond random acts when he pours out his kindness on those he loves.

When you give your heart to him, kindness becomes a way of life for you, because your realization of his eternal and intentional kindness toward you makes any other response impossible. Your kindness, a reflection of his to you, touches strangers and permeates your deepest relationships. It demonstrates its presence in the countless acts of caring and words you offer in support and encouragement to others.

Dear God: Each day, help me choose kindness in my dealings with others, remembering the extraordinary kindness you have shown me. Amen.

The mountains may be taken away and the hills may shake, but My loving-kindness will not be taken from you.

Isaiah 54:10 NLV

IN GOD'S PRESENCE

The Lord is beside you to help you.

Psalm 110:5 NCV

here is never a time when you are not with God. He is infinitely aware of your every move, thought, desire, and request. Still, one of the greatest joys you can ever experience is being in God's presence— those special moments when he seems closer, when the answers you receive from him profoundly affect you.

In times like this, you feel as if you are sitting at God's feet, listening to his every word with a heart of intense devotion and peace.

The psalmist learned that there was joy, wisdom, and strength to be gained by drawing near to God. Have you? Have you experienced the wonder of his presence

God, I am listening. Help me to experience your awesome presence and mold my life into a vessel of honor that will draw others to you in a personal way. Amen.

and the depth of his peace? Have you surrendered yourself to him and opened your heart to his eternal love? You should—because there is no better place to be.

Your people will offer themselves willingly in the day of Your power, in the beauty of holiness.

Psalm 110:3 AMP

TOGETHER WITH HIM

We're telling you so you can experience it along with us, this experience of communion with the Father and his Son, Jesus Christ.

1 John 1:3 THE MESSAGE

When Jesus walked on earth, he demonstrated his desire to forge close and lasting bonds with his people. Through their New Testament accounts, women and men privileged to follow him reach out to believers now, inviting all to experience the fellowship they enjoyed with him.

Dear God:
Help me respond to your fellowship by gladly sharing my experience with others so they, too, may draw close to you. Amen.

God's Spirit opens you to the spiritual union he yearns to establish between you and him, and he makes it possible for you to follow him. As you read through the Bible, you hear him speak on subjects of everyday life and teach on topics of eternal significance. Your fellowship with him compels you to invite others to experience the communion you have with God.

God will do this, for he is faithful to do what he says, and he has invited you into partnership with his Son, Jesus Christ our Lord.

1 Corinthians 1:9 NLT

LIFE AS HIS VESSEL

*He put a new song in my mouth, a song of praise to our God.
Many people will see this and worship him. Then they will
trust the Lord.*

Psalm 40:3 NCV

*I*t is generally easier to believe the negative things
people say about you rather than the positive. *Ugly.
Stupid. Disgraceful. Worthless.* These words make lasting
wounds on your heart, and it is difficult
to overcome them.

Yet remember, it is not what the vessel
is made of that gives it value but what it
contains. When you believe in God, he
fills you, and your life becomes a vessel of
praise to him. You have been completely
changed. You no longer have any reason
to feel shame, because God has provided
you with a new identity based on his
beauty, wisdom, holiness, and worth.

*God, you have changed
me from inside out,
and I praise your
name! Thank you for
giving me such hope,
worth, beauty, wisdom,
and holiness. Amen.*

Friend, you have been emptied of your indignities and filled with
God's glory. Let him shine through you so others can trust him as well.

Let all who seek you rejoice and be glad because of you. Let those who love
your salvation continually say, "The Lord is great!"

Psalm 40:16 GOD'S WORD

GOOD TIMES PAST

My heart is breaking as I remember how it used to be: I walked among the crowds of worshipers, leading a great procession to the house of God.

Psalm 42:4 NLT

Can you think of a time when your relationship with God felt deeper and more meaningful? Maybe you remember when your faith was new and his presence seemed to permeate your every activity.

Yet understand, it is dangerous to enshrine experiences with God, believing your best times with him are past. Your relationship with God is not just about what happened yesterday but about how you love and obey him today.

> *God, I want our relationship to be healthy and flourish. Help me to seek you daily so our intimacy can grow deeper all the days of my life. Amen.*

Although you should be encouraged by how God has helped you previously, you simply cannot base your entire relationship with him on the "good ole days." He certainly does not. So keep your eyes fixed on him always, and you will experience a more intimate relationship than you ever thought possible.

Why are you down in the dumps, dear soul? Why are you crying the blues? Fix my eyes on God—soon I'll be praising again. He puts a smile on my face. He's my God.

Psalm 42:5 THE MESSAGE

October 28

POWER OF GENTLENESS

Be gentle with one another, sensitive.
Ephesians 4:32 THE MESSAGE

Many women dismiss the quality of gentleness as an outmoded virtue impractical in today's world where they earn their own living, work alongside men, seek promotions, and negotiate the purchase price of their house and car. No one knows better than God the realities of your life, and he still calls you to wrap yourself in gentleness. Jesus, God's supreme example of gentleness, possessed all the powers of God, yet chose compassion, forgiveness, and tenderness in his dealings with humble women and men.

> *Heavenly Father:*
> *Grant me sensitivity*
> *to the needs of*
> *others as well as a*
> *compassionate heart*
> *and temperate tongue.*
> *Let your Spirit enable*
> *me to practice the*
> *power of gentleness.*
> *Amen.*

In Jesus, you have your mentor, and every reason to bring into the twenty-first century the quality of godly gentleness as a positive attribute.

Your gentleness has made me great.
Psalm 18:35 NKJV

HEAVENLY JOY

God's kingdom . . . [is] what God does with your life as he sets it right, puts it together, and completes it with joy.

Romans 14:17 THE MESSAGE

As a little child, you may have pictured heaven as a far-away place with beautiful angels floating around castles that glittered in the sun. You were correct in thinking that heaven is a realm of breathtaking beauty, but through God's Spirit, it isn't so very far away.

God brings the beauty of heaven to you as his Spirit works peace, joy, loveliness, and goodness in your heart. Day by day, your God-pleasing thoughts, words, and actions increasingly transform you into a woman of transcendent beauty, a woman in whom God's Spirit lives and breathes, a woman who enjoys the sweet closeness of heaven right here on Earth.

Heavenly Father: Open my heart to the work of your Spirit in me, and allow me to live each day in your love. Amen.

God's kingdom is within you.

Luke 17:21 NCV

GLAD PRAISE

Ascribe to the Lord the glory due his name; worship the Lord in the splendor of his holiness.

Psalm 29:2 NIV

You make time for and look forward to an activity you truly enjoy, and God wants you to approach worship the same way. He opens the doors of his heart for you. Enter with anticipation and expectation that he, your host, will be pleased with your praise and thanksgiving.

Visualize yourself standing in the presence of your God and King with a light heart and broad smile, soaking up his goodness, basking in his love. Allow your voice to rise in response, whether in song or with simple words, and make it your own special gift. Then make time for and look forward to your next worship opportunity.

Heavenly Father: I am grateful for all the opportunities I have to worship you, and my heart responds with gladness at the privilege of standing in your presence. Amen.

Thank him. Worship him. For god is sheer beauty, all-generous in love, loyal always and ever.

Psalm 100:4–5 THE MESSAGE

October 31

ANSWERS FROM
UNEXPECTED PLACES

God made water flow from rocks he split open in the desert, and his people drank freely, as though from a lake. He made streams gush out like rivers from rocks.

Psalm 78:15–16 CEV

ere is one of the most exciting things about God: he does not always answer your prayers the same way. Just when you think you understand how he will solve a problem, he takes a different route. This is why having faith is so important.

Always make sure that whatever you are doing is in line with the principles of his Word, but also allow him to be God—submit to him whenever he reshapes your plans even when you do not comprehend why he is leading you in a certain way. Never try to box him in with your expectations.

Because you will find that when you think you know all there is to know about him, he will do something far better than you could have ever imagined. In addition, that is when you are truly blessed.

God, I love the way you surprise me with your goodness. Help me to always remain hopeful—anticipating your answers from unexpected places. Amen.

They remembered that God was their rock, that the Most High was their defender.

Psalm 78:35 GOD'S WORD

NOVEMBER

*My peace I give you. I do not
give to you as the world gives.
Do not let your hearts be troubled
and do not be afraid.*

JOHN 14:27 NIV

November 1

THE SOURCE OF SUCCESS

Not from the east nor from the west nor from the south come promotion and lifting up. But God is the Judge! He puts down one and lifts up another.

Psalm 75:6–7 AMP

God waits for the perfect time to work. Up until the moment you see him in action, you may fear he's forgotten the situations that weigh so heavily on your heart. However, be assured that he knows exactly what he is doing—and success is forthcoming.

> *Lord, forgive me for the times that I forget that you are omniscient and aware of all that is taking place. I know you will accomplish your will. Amen.*

In time, you will see how he has been working in the unseen. However, his instruction to you right now is a simple command to be steadfast and true to him. In other words, do not forfeit your faith. Even though you do not see the evidence of his hand at work, he is wholeheartedly committed to honoring his promises to you.

God has a plan, and at the right moment, you will see it unfold. He will work all things together for your good in due time.

God says, "I will break the strength of the wicked, but I will increase the power of the godly."

Psalm 75:10 NLT

November 2

TRUE FREEDOM

God can be trusted not to let you be tempted too much, and he will show you how to escape from your temptations.

1 Corinthians 10:13 CEV

*A*s you understand more about God's love for you, you may find yourself becoming more aware of temptations in your life that do not fit in with his purpose for you.

It pleases God when you tell him about the appeal these things may have for you. He cares and understands, and will help you overcome their allure. You will walk away from them stronger than before. Your urges and earthly desires do not possess the kind of power God has, and he promises to give his power to you. God created you to be free, and he doesn't want you to give that freedom away to anyone or anything.

Be strong in the Lord and in his mighty power.

Ephesians 6:10 NLT

Dear God: Remove the barriers in front of me. I need your strength and power to keep on your path of peace, goodness, and joy. Amen.

November 3

YOUR SOUL'S
TRUE YEARNING

My soul thirsts for God, for the living God. When shall I come and appear before God?

Psalm 42:2 NKJV

*Y*ou cannot seem to fill that uneasy longing within. You go shopping, but it doesn't help. You eat something delicious, but that does not satisfy you either. You try socializing more to fill the emptiness, but soon you find that doesn't do it either.

It isn't your body, heart, or stomach that is crying out, it is your soul. It is the part of you that requires spiritual growth and refreshment. Friend, you need God. You need God more than you need food, clothing, sunshine, or shelter. Your Creator satisfies your yearning for purpose, worth, and eternity, teaching you his insight and inspiring you with his presence.

Neither the spoon nor the credit card can help you, but prayer and reading his Word can. So do not ignore this crucial need. Your thirst is for God. Drink and be filled.

The Lord will send His faithful love by day; His song will be with me in the night—a prayer to the God of my life.

Psalm 42:8 HCSB

God, thank you for satisfying the deep needs of my soul—for inspiring me with your purpose and refreshing me with you presence. You truly fill me with joy. Amen.

November 4

THE SILENT TREATMENT

O Lord my Rock, be not deaf and silent to me. . . . Hear the voice of my supplication as I cry to You for help.

Psalm 28:1–2 AMP

*Y*ou need answers, so you humble yourself before God's throne and listen. However, there is no response. There is not even the hint of a reply.

There is only silence.

Repeatedly you pray, wondering why he has not addressed your pleas, searching your soul to see if you have done anything wrong. Your ears strain for a word. Soon your quest is no longer about getting an answer. You just want to hear his voice. Friend, that is exactly where you need to be.

God, please do not let me miss your instruction. Rather, help me to keep seeking you even when you are silent — because you mean everything to me. Amen.

Has God been quiet lately? He may be waiting until your sole desire is his presence in your life. Your best course is to keep seeking and loving him. Because when he does finally answer, it is going to be a very important message, and you will not want to miss it.

The Lord is my strength and my shield; in him my heart trusts, and I am helped; my heart exults, and with my song I give thanks to him.

Psalm 28:7 ESV

ALL GOOD THINGS

See if I will not open the windows of heaven for you and pour down for you an overflowing blessing.

Malachi 3:10 NRSV

*Y*ou may have heard the saying "All things in moderation." While it is good advice for our own conduct, it isn't God's way of doing things. With his many and varied blessings, he's downright extravagant.

God has provided a world of sunshine and starshine, fields and seas, rivers and mountains. He has blessed you with life and breath, with thoughts, abilities, and a heart turned toward knowing and loving him. Thank him, and he says, "My beloved, you haven't seen anything yet. There is so much more!"

There's no end to what God can and wants to do. With all good things, God is a God of abundance.

Dear God: Thank you for the good things you have put into my life today. Keep me eternally thankful for everything I receive. Amen.

May his blessings and peace be yours, sent to you from God our Father and Jesus Christ our Lord.

Ephesians 1:2 TLB

GUARDING YOUR ATTITUDE

O God the Lord, the strength of my salvation, You have covered my head in the day of battle.

Psalm 140:7 NASB

*N*othing causes a more decisive defeat than a negative attitude. When you are confronted with a challenge and imagine it is absolutely impossible to overcome, you have already lost the battle. This will happen whenever you measure the troubles in your life against your own capabilities.

When your focus is on God's ability to help you, you have already won the victory. You cling to the fact that he protects you, provides for you, and will empower you to prevail over anything you face. This knowledge gives you the courage you need for the challenge ahead.

So guard your thoughts by covering them with God's truth. Obey him. Trust him. Never allow anything to distract you from his wonderful grace. Because surely he will lead you to triumph.

God, please protect me from negativity. Cover my mind with the Bible—make it sink in and give me hope. With you is the victory, so I will fix my thoughts on you. Amen.

Surely the righteous shall give thanks to Your name; the upright shall dwell in Your presence.

Psalm 140:13 NKJV

FOLLOW IN FAITH

We walk by faith, not by sight.
2 Corinthians 5:7 NKJV

She wanted to learn how to make a quilt, so she bought a book on quilting. How each step contributed to the finished quilt was not always clear to her, but she followed the instructions and completed a beautiful work of art.

Dear God:
Grant me the desire and willingness to walk in faith and follow the Bible's teachings so that I may rejoice in the fulfillment of all your promises. Amen.

As you continue to walk with God, some steps along the way may seem unclear, and that's when God asks you to proceed in faith. He shows you his plan—ultimately life with him in heaven—and in the Bible he gives you his step-by-step instructions on how to get there and live a God-pleasing life along the way.

Continue in faith, and God promises you a beautiful result.

Faith is the substance of things hoped for, the evidence of things not seen.

Hebrews 11:1 NKJV

BELIEVING THE BIBLE

He saved them for his name's sake, that he might make known his mighty power. . . . Then they believed his words; they sang his praise.

Psalm 106:8, 12 ESV

*P*erhaps you've wondered: *What if I make the wrong choice? What if I make a terrible mistake?* You have stayed awake at night pondering the right way to handle some difficult decision, and you are fraught with anxiety.

God knows all that you are facing, and he knows how you should handle the situation. Will he help you with the decision that you need to make? Will he show you how to make the right choice? The answer is yes, when you ask him to show you what is best and you believe him.

He may speak to you through the Bible or through a trusted Christian friend, but you must trust and obey him when he speaks. So be still, listen for his answer to your prayers, and be confident that he will lead you in the right way.

God, I greatly admire your power. I am amazed how you never become weary or tired of teaching me how to live each day. I believe you, God. Lead me. Amen.

Hallelujah! Give thanks to the Lord, for He is good; His faithful love endures forever. Who can declare the Lord's mighty acts or proclaim all the praise due Him?

Psalm 106:1–2 HCSB

THE BASIS FOR YOUR TRUST

Ascribe to the Lord glory and strength. Give to the Lord the glory due to His name; worship the Lord in the beauty of holiness.

Psalm 29:1–2 AMP

You have been encouraged to trust God; but why should you be confident in his care? How can you depend upon someone you have never seen?

Understand that your faith in God is not to be blind or unsubstantiated. Rather, it should be based on his faultless character. He is all-powerful, completely able to do whatever is necessary to help you. He is all-knowing; his wisdom concerning your situation and how to deliver you is flawless. He will only do what is in your absolute best interest.

Friend, what challenge weighs on your heart today? Trust God to help you. You have great reason for confidence because of his wonderful character. So do as he says, because he is willing and able to bring you the victory.

God, you are so worthy of praise and adoration. I thank you for your faultless character and great help to me. I am truly blessed by your love. Amen.

Above the floodwaters is God's throne from which his power flows, from which he rules the world. God makes his people strong. God gives his people peace.

Psalm 29:10–11 THE MESSAGE

SWEET SOLITUDE

In quietness and confidence shall be your strength.
Isaiah 30:15 NKJV

To find a place of stillness and soul-nurturing solitude, you do not need to plan a retreat in the woods or isolate yourself in a secluded cabin. Just look within yourself. God's Spirit, dwelling in you, has fixed a shelter for your soul, a place of peace where you can delight in being alone with him.

Achieving a quiet heart and mind takes practice, as anyone following the contemplative life will tell you. Start with a few minutes of quiet time, focusing your thoughts on God, and then gradually add more time to your meditation. Learn to rest in his peace and enjoy the sweetness of his solitude.

*Heavenly Father:
Draw me ever closer
to you by teaching me
how to quiet my mind
and wait in patient
attendance on you.
Amen.*

Be still, and know that I am God.
Psalm 46:10 NIV

AN EXPERT ABOUT YOU

O Lord, you have examined me, and you know me. . . . You are familiar with all my ways.

No one understands you better than God—he knows you even better than you know yourself. He has a perfect, complete knowledge about you that is not bound by time or human limitations.

He loves you.

God, I praise you for creating me and knowing all my life can be. Thank you for loving me and leading me in the very best way possible. I know I can trust you. Amen.

Whenever you begin to think that no one appreciates the pressures you face, remember that God does. He recognizes how each trial affects you and how each challenge molds your character.

God is an expert about you and all your life can be—and he will not allow one area of potential in you to go unexplored if you will obey him.

Have faith in your Creator and trust him to lead you to the abundant life he formed you for. Certainly, he has amazing blessings planned for you. Seek him first and foremost.

Search me [thoroughly], O God, and know my heart! Try me and know my thoughts! And see if there is any wicked or hurtful way in me, and lead me in the way everlasting.

Psalm 139:23–24 AMP

YOU ARE NOT ALONE

If we live in the light, as God is in the light, we can share fellow-ship with each other.

1 John 1:7 NCV

As you walk forward in your relationship with God, it's important to spend time with others who share your faith. Churches, women's Bible study groups, service projects, and social circles all provide opportunities. You may be surprised how quickly you bond and how deep and lasting your re-lationships become. After all, you share a secret, the greatest love of all!

> *Heavenly Father: Help me to find friends who are women of faith. Grant me many opportunities to join in fellowship with them. Amen.*

Surround yourself with women who love and respect God and you will soon find they can be a source of true wisdom and spiritual encouragement. Your heav-enly Father never intended that you walk the life of faith alone, but rather with other women who will love and support you.

Love the brothers and sisters of God's family.

1 Peter 2:17 NCV

THE DARK BEFORE DAYLIGHT

At night we may cry, but when morning comes we will celebrate.

Psalm 30:5 CEV

The hour is late, and you are exhausted. Anxiety is keeping you awake even though you realize you cannot fix things, at least not right now. The tears flow. How can you live another day with this problem hanging over you? The situation seems as dark and hopeless as the night sky.

Friend, you simply cannot continue without rest. Your weariness is making your actions less effective and your situation appear more dismal. You need to sleep, to recuperate your mental, emotional, and physical strength. Understandably, it will take faith for you to shut your eyes; however, God will continue providing for you even while you slumber.

God, please calm my fears and give me rest. I want to trust you, Lord. Please release me from these worries so I can praise your matchless name. Amen.

Therefore, rest in him. Expect him to work on your behalf. Because no matter how dire the situation, he can restore your joy. Trust him.

You have changed my sadness into a joyful dance. . . . So I will not be silent; I will sing praise to you. Lord, you are my God; I will give you thanks forever.

Psalm 30:11–12 GNT

HE'S NEVER LATE

Be patient . . . until the Lord's coming.

James 5:7 NIV

"The patience of Job" didn't apply to his wife, for as Job endured extraordinary trials, she saw only his wretchedness and even advised her husband to give up the struggle and die. Though the Bible says Job cried out to God in his distress, he did not give up, viewing his trials through the lens of eternity.

God opens his ears to your cries and his arms when you are hurt, and above all, he opens your eyes so you can see things from his perspective. When you place this moment against all eternity, your Spirit-given patience deepens because you see God bringing all things to pass, and he is never late.

Dear God: When I feel frustrated, send your Spirit into my heart and grant me patience to endure, relying on you to work each situation out in your own time. Amen.

God will strengthen you with his own great power. And you will not give up when troubles come, but you will be patient.

Colossians 1:11 ICB

A HELPING HAND

Jesus said, "Here is a simple, rule-of-thumb guide for behavior: Ask yourself what you want people to do for you, then grab the initiative and do it for them."

Matthew 7:12 THE MESSAGE

In your sincere desire to help others, do you sometimes find yourself wondering if getting involved would violate a friend's privacy or undermine a neighbor's right to make her own decisions? It can be unsettling.

Jesus offers his perspective when he invites you to take a few moments to imagine yourself in the place of the other person. After reflecting on her fears, struggles, abilities, and resources, consider what you would most appreciate someone doing for you. Then confidently do the same thing for her.

Dear God: Grant me a heart of wisdom so I may reach out to others in genuinely helpful and caring ways. Amen.

Sometimes your act will be the perfect response and sometimes it won't, but every time you will be passing along the message that God cares.

Because of [Christ] all the parts of the body care for each other and help each other.

Colossians 2:19 ICB

REFLECTING HIS CHARACTER

Happy are those who are concerned for the poor; the Lord will help them when they are in trouble.

Psalm 41:1 GNT

God has provided everything you have. When you needed salvation, he gave it to you freely. When you were desperate for his help and comfort, he sent it to you without reservation.

He does this not only for your sake, but for those around you as well. You see, it is his desire that as you receive his compassion and encouragement, they will transform you and you will grow in his character. You become kindhearted and giving as a result of your love and gratitude to the Lord.

Friend, do you give freely, reflecting God's character and provision to others? God is generous and loving, and he wants his people to be so as well. So today be his representative and care for those in need just as he would.

> *God, thank you for your mercy and generosity. Help me to meet others' needs with your sincere compassion so that they can know you and praise your name. Amen.*

By this I know that You favor and delight in me. . . . You have upheld me in my integrity and set me in Your presence forever.

Psalm 41:11–12 AMP

HIS COMFORTING HAND

I serve you, Lord. Comfort me with your love, just as you have promised.

Psalm 119:76 CEV

As women, we spend a lot of time comforting others. But what happens when we need to be comforted? God is always there, reaching out his hand, calming us, reassuring us, loving us.

You need only to place yourself in God's strong, capable hands. Maybe you need to feel his presence alongside you when your spirit is tested by grief or sorrow. Is your body aching or your troubled mind screaming for relief? God is there for you—today, tomorrow, and the next day. Do not be afraid to cry out to him. The Bible says your tears are precious to him. Let him comfort you.

Dear God: I have no one to turn to but you. Thank you for never leaving my side in the good times and the bad. Amen.

You keep track of all my sorrows. You have collected all my tears in your bottle. You have recorded each one in your book.

Psalm 56:8 NLT

PROACTIVE OR REACTIVE?

We will tell to the generation to come the praiseworthy deeds of the Lord, and His might, and the wonderful works that He has performed.

Psalm 78:4 AMP

Your life is a testimony of the way God works. People will learn whether they can truly trust the Lord by observing how you handle moments of joy as well as times of sorrow.

Friend, when you battle hardships and obstacles, do you still demonstrate faith in your unshakable God? There were times when Moses, David, Paul, and the disciples experienced terrible pressure. However, each one of them refused to give up or react negatively to their circumstances.

Rather, they were proactive—they not only honored the Lord and grew in their faith, but many others came to know him through their excellent example.

The same can be true for you, but you must decide to trust him in every situation. Will you honor him no matter what happens? Will you be his faithful witness as well?

Lord, I choose to trust you today and refuse to believe or respond to any and every thought of spiritual defeat.

He commanded our fathers, that they should make them known to their children . . . that they may set their hope in God, and not forget the works of God, but keep His commandments.

Psalm 78:5, 7 NKJV

WORTH EVERYTHING

I have called you by name; you are mine.

Isaiah 43:1 NLT

The daughter of migrant farm workers, a girl's time in the classroom depended on how long her parents worked in a particular place. She dreamed of a better life, and with the help of caring educators, she eventually earned a college degree.

Though obstacles may hinder your desire to enjoy the peace of mind God offers, to mature in faith, and become the woman God wants you to be, God acts as your caring counselor. He is committed to seeing you become all you can be, and he sends his Spirit to convince you of his ongoing care for you.

As a daughter of God, you are worth everything to him.

Heavenly Father: Help me to see myself in your eyes as a woman precious to you, and help me respond by making my life a testament to your love. Amen.

Before I shaped you in the womb, I knew all about you. Before you saw the light of day, I had holy plans for you.

Jeremiah 1:5 THE MESSAGE

TOUGH WORLD, TENDER GOD

You have seen my troubles, and you care about the anguish of my soul. You have not handed me over to my enemies but have set me in a safe place.

Psalm 31:7–8 NLT

Trouble comes in many forms and finds everyone eventually. Some people feel like outcasts and never really learn to fit in. Others face financial, physical, or relational problems that keep them in constant chaos. The world offers no solutions or mercy. On the contrary, people must constantly beware of those who would take advantage of their weaknesses.

Unfortunately, instead of turning to God, people question why he allows so much suffering. Yet the reason there is such turmoil is that sin is a painful reality in the world.

Friend, God longs to show you his loving care, but you must stop clinging to the world and blaming him for your hardships. Rather, embrace him. He will reveal the truth and free you from your hurt.

Be strong, all who wait with hope for the Lord, and let your heart be courageous.

Psalm 31:24 GOD's WORD

God, forgive me for blaming you for my troubles and turning to the world for comfort. Help me to always remember that only you can truly heal my heart. Amen.

WHEN IT'S DIFFICULT TO PRAISE

How shall we sing the Lord's song in a strange land?

Psalm 137:4 AMP

hen the inhabitants of Jerusalem were taken captive to Babylon, they lost absolutely everything. Their homes, families, and even the temple where they worshiped God were all completely destroyed. It was as if their identity and security had been lost forever. How could they possibly praise?

Perhaps you're experiencing a similar loss—your life's been destroyed and you don't know what to do.

God, it is difficult, but I praise you for your past goodness to me and your faithfulness throughout history. I look forward to your deliverance and restoration. Amen.

First, you must remember all the times God has been faithful to you in the past. Second, cling to the fact that God is still with you and is working on your behalf—no matter how the circumstances may appear.

God eventually brought the people back to Jerusalem and enabled them to rebuild the temple. He will restore you as well. Look forward to that time and praise him—for he will certainly help you.

Let my tongue stick to the roof of my mouth if I do not remember you, if I do not think about Jerusalem as my greatest joy.

Psalm 137:6 NCV

KNOWING HIM IS ETERNAL

This is eternal life, that they know you the only true God, and Jesus Christ whom you have sent.

John 17:3 ESV

There will be times in your life when your only source of comfort will be God. It will be through worship, prayer, and Bible study that you gain the energy, wisdom, and hope to make it through the day.

This is not a trial, this is the goal—to need no earthly encouragement because God has become everything to you. Your comfort, peace, and joy all come from God. It is during these times that God replaces your earthly nature with a love and longing for the eternal.

I thank you, God, that learning about you today is about loving you in countless tomorrows. I love you and praise your wonderful name. Amen.

Rejoice. God is preparing you for eternal life by changing your perspective and helping you to know him better.

Build yourselves up in your most holy faith; pray in the Holy Spirit; keep yourselves in the love of God, waiting for the mercy of our Lord Jesus Christ that leads to eternal life.

Jude 1:20–21 ESV

AN AMAZING FUTURE

You, Lord God, have done many wonderful things, and you have planned marvelous things for us. No one is like you! I would never be able to tell all you have done.

Psalm 40:5 CEV

This verse contains a wonderful promise: God has planned marvelous things for you. In fact, his vision for your future is infinitely higher and abundantly better than anything you could imagine.

If you are somewhat confused about what he is doing in your life—it is no wonder. You are not supposed to figure it out or understand how all of your experiences fit together. Not yet, anyway. God is doing something through you that is so amazing it can only be achieved by his magnificent power and imagination.

God, I can imagine some amazing things—but your plans are resplendently filled with your love, power, and brilliance. Praise your wonderful name! Amen.

Allow this hope to strengthen you today: Because of God's extraordinary love, the best is still ahead. His plans for your future are unfolding, and they are truly fantastic. So have faith, friend, honor him always, and praise his glorious name.

I delight to do Your will, O my God; Your Law is within my heart.

Psalm 40:8 NASB

GIFT OF FORGIVENESS

Bear with one another and, if anyone has a complaint against another, forgive each other; just as the Lord has forgiven you, so you also must forgive.

Colossians 3:13 NRSV

God has provided complete forgiveness through the work of Christ, and now he asks you to follow his example when it comes to those who have hurt you.

In his earthly ministry, Jesus Christ bore the insults of his persecutors without returning insult for insult, and he uttered words of forgiveness even to the soldiers nailing him to the cross. He never considered whether the person deserved forgiveness; he simply forgave, because his compassionate heart allowed no other response.

Take pleasure in living as the completely forgiven woman of God you are, and let your heart of compassion deal mercifully with those in need of your pardon.

> *Heavenly Father: In gratitude for the gift of your forgiveness, move me to choose forgiveness instead of offense when dealing with the failings of others. Amen.*

Love prospers when a fault is forgiven.

Proverbs 17:9 NLT

AN OUTPOURING
OF BEAUTY

Sing for joy in the Lord, O you righteous ones; praise is becoming to the upright.

Psalm 33:1 NASB

Would you consider yourself beautiful? Every culture has its standards for attractiveness; yet there are character attributes that are seen as universally lovely in every society.

A woman who is loving, joyful, peaceful, patient, kind, good, faithful, gentle, and self-controlled is regarded as exquisite all over the world.

That is because these are traits created in you by God's Holy Spirit. They flow from you effortlessly when you live your life in obedience and adoration to him.

Would you like to be considered truly lovely? Then remember that you are most attractive when you are praising him and letting his beauty shine through you. Moreover, when his radiance covers you, you are stunning no matter where you go.

God, thank you for making me radiant with your beauty! May adoration and praise flow from my life so all will worship you. Amen.

Sing to Him a new song; play skillfully [on the strings] with a loud and joyful sound. For the word of the Lord is right; and all His work is done in faithfulness.

Psalm 33:3–4 AMP

GOOD-BYE TO GUILT

I confessed my sins and told them all to you. I said, "I'll tell the Lord each one of my sins." Then you forgave me and took away my guilt.

Psalm 32:5 CEV

There are those who believe that humanity is inherently flawed, and in a sense, they are right. Sin corrupts from within, and people are powerless to break its influence over them.

Thankfully, you are not without hope. Though you cannot help yourself, you know the One who erases your guilt and releases you from its bondage. The problem you have, is letting go. You somehow convince yourself that the wickedness within you is more than Christ can handle. However, that simply is not true.

Friend, if you are seeking freedom from the destructive power of sin, there is only one way to find it—and that's through Jesus Christ. Stop trying to earn what he has offered you freely. Instead, embrace the good he wants to do in and through you and say good-bye to your guilt.

God, thank you for forgiving me of my sins. You have released me from my guilt and given me a clean heart. I praise your holy and powerful name! Amen.

You are my hiding place; You shall preserve me from trouble; You shall surround me with songs of deliverance.

Psalm 32:7 NKJV

SAFETY FIRST

[My people] will live in safety, and no one will frighten them.

Ezekiel 34:28 NLT

Safety becomes a primary concern when a woman examines toys for her young children or helps her elderly parents choose an apartment. Similarly, God has your safety in mind as he guides you on the path of life.

God keeps you safe from harmful influences by reminding you not only of his love for you, but of the purpose he has for you. He keeps you secure in the knowledge of your status as a beloved woman of God, and he establishes in you the Spirit-grown conviction that you have nothing to fear.

Dear God: Help me find my sole security in you and your divine purpose for my life. I rest at ease in the strong shelter of your love. Amen.

Privileged to live a life of meaning and purpose, rest securely in him.

The beloved of the Lord rests in safety.

Deuteronomy 33:12 NRSV

November 28

OUT OF TROUBLE

They cried to the Lord in their trouble, and he saved them from their distress. He brought them out of darkness and the deepest gloom and broke away their chains.

Psalm 107:13–14 NIV

*H*ave you ever felt like giving up? Most people have. The truth is, if you live long enough, you will battle thoughts of discouragement, but you do not have to give in to them. There is hope even when the landscape of your life appears dark and stormy. The psalmist cried out to God, and he was saved from his distress.

What was the key to his turnaround? He acknowledged his situation to God and proclaimed his faith in God. Instead of being "me focused," he was God focused. When you are tempted to keep going, pushing to resolve a difficult issue—stop. Go to God in prayer and cry out to him. You will find that clouds of disheartenment quickly evaporate in his presence.

He sent His word and healed them, and delivered them from their destructions.

Psalm 107:20 NASB

God, I know there are times when I have not trusted you fully, and have been discouraged because of it. Forgive me, God, and help me to have hope in you. Amen.

GOOD FEAR?

You alone must be feared!
Psalm 76:7 GOD'S WORD

he sense of fear the psalmist is writing about is a reverent fear that honors God. It has nothing to do with being so frightened that you turn and run away from him.

Jesus, thank you for forgiving my sin and for teaching me the holy reverence that leads to salvation. Help me to always rest in your care and holy presence. Amen.

Adam and Eve hid because they had disobeyed God. They were afraid he was going to punish them, because sin always demands a payment for the wrong that has been done.

Jesus Christ paid the ultimate price for your sin at the cross. You do not have to hide from him or anxiously wait for him to punish you. When you seek him, he faithfully forgives and restores you immediately.

God never wants you to dread his presence; rather, he wants the respect that grows from love. Therefore, fear him—in the good way. Because that is the fear that leads to salvation.

All who live on this earth were terrified and silent when you took over as judge, ready to rescue everyone in need.

Psalm 76:8–9 CEV

November 30

FOUNTAIN OF YOUTH

You have clothed yourselves with a brand new nature that is continually being renewed as you learn more and more about Christ.

Colossians 3:10 NLT

Noticing the first gray hair or confronting a few laugh lines in the mirror, we acknowledge, usually with a sigh, we're not getting any younger. At the same time, God restores, renews, and rejuvenates our spiritual lives through the work of his Spirit within us.

Because of your faith, God continually restores your relationship with him by offering you absolute forgiveness. In your soul, God's Spirit renews your commitment to follow him and rejuvenates your faith, empowering you to overcome challenges and obstacles along the way.

Dear God: I need the spiritual refreshment you offer through faith, forgiveness, and commitment to follow you through all the days and stages of my life. Amen.

Relax and enjoy God's antidote for aging—restoration, renewal, and rejuvenation in him.

We are being renewed day by day.
2 Corinthians 4:16 NIV

DECEMBER

Happy are those who find wisdom,
and those who get understanding,
for her income is better than silver,
and her revenue better than gold.

PROVERBS 3:13—14 NRSV

YOUR HAVEN IN HIM

They were glad when it grew calm, and he guided them to their desired haven.

Psalm 107:30 NIV

One of the irresistible things about God is how he often gives you the desires of your heart. When your life is fully committed to him, he blesses you. This is because the closer you are to him, the more you realize the things of the world are unworthy of your attention. Rather, you want to enjoy his pleasures.

God, I love to know you better — not just so I can receive your good gifts, but also so I can truly know and enjoy you more. You are my peaceful place of refuge. Amen.

You will also notice that the more you surrender your life to him, the more you sense his personal care for you. You experience his blessings in a new way, and may even begin to wonder what you have done to receive so much from him.

That is the way he is—God gives good things to his children. When your life is committed to him, he provides for every need you have and much more.

He hushes the storm to a calm and to a gentle whisper, so that the waves of the sea are still.

Psalm 107:29 AMP

December 2

LIFE'S PURPOSE

Lead a life worthy of the calling to which you have been called.

Ephesians 4:1 NRSV

rom early childhood, some girls know what they want to do in life, and when they grow up, they do it. But most of us need time to discover our life's work, and we might even take several detours before we find our way.

God created you with a specific purpose in mind, and he has endowed you with all the gifts, talents, resources, and opportunities you need to live out his plan for your life. If the course ahead appears unclear to you, rest easy. When you place your trust in his wisdom and in his love, you're pointed in the right direction. You will find what you seek.

Heavenly Father: At every stage in my life, direct me and guide me according to your good and gracious will. Amen.

We are His workmanship, created in Christ Jesus for good works, which God prepared beforehand that we should walk in them.

Ephesians 2:10 NKJV

A DIFFERENT FOCUS

Lord, make me to know my end and [to appreciate] the measure of my days—what it is; let me know and realize how frail I am [how transient is my stay here].

Psalm 39:4 AMP

oo often people base their happiness on a future experience—a career, a wedding, the birth of a child, or what have you. They are utterly convinced that they will not be content or complete without it. Unfortunately, they are so focused on tomorrow that they fail to make the most of today, and they miss the blessings God has for them.

Friend, is this you? Are you waiting for life to begin when you get that great job, meet the perfect man, or achieve some other goal? Then your focus is misplaced.

God has important things for you to do and people for you to love today. So do not waste your life on fantasies. Rather, devote it to the One who will make you truly joyful and whole. The rest will come in its time.

God, only you can truly make my life meaningful. Please help me to focus on honoring you today rather than the blessings of tomorrow. Amen.

Lord, what do I wait for? My hope is in You.

Psalm 39:7 HCSB

December 4

SWEET DREAMS

If you sit down, you will not be afraid; when you lie down, your sleep will be sweet.

Proverbs 3:24 NRSV

The benefits of a sufficient amount of sleep include better physical health, increased mental acuity, greater emotional control, and general well-being. While the benefits are well known, few women say they regularly enjoy a good night's sleep.

God makes it possible for you to get a good night's sleep by removing those things that keep you awake. He lifts your cares from you, and he hears your words of thanksgiving for the blessings of your day, of confession for the errors of the day, and your words of trust in him for a fresh start tomorrow. Do this, and sleep peacefully all the hours your body and soul require.

> *Dear God: Help me commit to enjoying a good night's sleep by making time for sleep and closing my day with a prayer of thanksgiving, confession, and trust. Amen.*

I will lie down and sleep in peace, O Lord, You alone keep me safe.

Psalm 4:8 NLV

WITH HISTORY AS A GUIDE

You are the God who works wonders; you have made known your might among the peoples.

Psalm 77:14 ESV

The Bible is full of stories of faith—of people trapped in terrible situations but who subsequently triumph because of the Lord.

Perhaps like them, you are facing a problem that seems overwhelming. Yet God knows exactly what you are facing, and he understands your fears. He knows when you feel tempted to give up and has promised never to abandon you. When you feel as though there is no place to turn, he provides a way of escape.

Just as he helped the saints throughout history, he can help you . Trust him. He is just as powerful, faithful, and wise today as when he delivered them, and surely he will give you the victory as well.

God, it is easy to trust you in times of sunshine, but help me to have faith in the storm by reminding me of your faithful works throughout the ages. Amen.

I will remember your great deeds, Lord; I will recall the wonders you did in the past. I will think about all that you have done; I will meditate on all your mighty acts.

Psalm 77:11–12 GNT

DON'T GIVE UP

*The Lord will fulfill his purpose for me; your steadfast love,
O Lord, endures forever.*

Psalm 138:8 ESV

At times, God will allow detours to the calling and dreams you've received from him. Perhaps you experience a major setback in an important goal or relationship. Maybe he has directed you in a way that seems counterintuitive. Whatever the case, you feel as if you are moving away from your heart's desire rather than toward it— and it is extremely disheartening.

> *God, thank you for my situation —even though it is confusing to me. I will cling wholeheartedly to you and trust you to fulfill your purpose for me. Amen.*

You may be tempted to give in to your discouragement, but don't. Remember, nothing can come into your life without first passing through God's permissive hand, because he is forming you for a unique purpose and a wonderful future.

You must express your confidence in him by patiently, steadfastly clinging to him and obeying his commands. In that way, you show him that you are ready for the assignments and blessings he has for you.

Though I walk in the midst of trouble, You will revive me; You will stretch forth Your hand . . . and Your right hand will save me.

Psalm 138:7 NASB

TOGETHER AS ONE

May the God who gives endurance and encouragement give you a spirit of unity among yourselves as you follow Christ Jesus.

Romans 15:5 NIV

A family living together in harmony and the family of believers worshiping together in peace meet God's intentions for his people. Good things happen when Christians come together in heart and mind—families become havens of encouragement, support, and affirmation, and congregations grow into models of true Christian unity.

Dear God: Put before my eyes your desire for all believers to journey together within the common embrace of Christian love. Amen.

God invites you to help implement his vision of unity in both your natural and your spiritual families. He sends his Spirit, empowering you to discover and develop areas of common interest and purpose, and he sets in front of you his ideal of a unified people of God, offering you an inspiring picture of the goal he has in mind.

How very good and pleasant it is when kindred live together in unity!

Psalm 133:1 NRSV

December 8

FULLY ACCEPTED

There is neither Jew nor Greek, there is neither slave nor free man, there is neither male nor female; for you are all one in Christ Jesus.

Galatians 3:28 NASB

Every woman knows that in this world not everyone is treated equally. It's a lesson she will learn again and again on her path through life. God has instituted a different standard in his kingdom; there are no distinctions, we all have equal standing before him.

What a wonderful thought to ponder. There are no limitations on your relationship with God. Your earthly social and cultural standing are of no importance to him. Your gender, your age, and your parentage are of no consequence to the ruler of heaven and earth. He accepts you fully and completely as you are. You can count on that.

Dear God: Thank you for seeing past all the extraneous criteria by which I am defined and accepting me completely for who I am. Amen.

He destined us for adoption as his children through Jesus Christ, according to the good pleasure of his will . . . his glorious grace that he freely bestowed on us.

Ephesians 1:5–6 NRSV

DO THE GODLY HAVE
BAD DAYS?

O Lord . . . my groaning has not been hidden from you. . . . I confess
my guilt. My sin troubles me.

Psalm 38:9, 18 GOD'S WORD

With so many promises and blessings that come with knowing God, one may get the false impression that there are no longer any trials or temptations for those who believe in him. However, that simply is not true.

God comprehends that you are not perfect. You are still going to make mistakes—dishonoring him and hurting yourself in the process. That does not mean you have ruined your relationship with him or forfeited your place in heaven. Rather, it means that you still have things to learn.

Friend, do not allow the guilt of a bad day to defeat you. Rather, repent of your mistake and accept it for what it is—an opportunity for God's grace and instruction. Then embrace what he teaches so that the next time temptation comes knocking, you can do what is right.

God, thank you for your patience with me, for picking me up when I fall, and for putting me back on the path to righteousness. Truly you are good. Amen.

What I do, God, is wait for you, wait for my Lord, my God—you will answer!

Psalm 38:15 THE MESSAGE

FEAR NOT

I sought the Lord, and he answered me and delivered me from all my fears.

Psalm 34:4 ESV

What are you afraid of? What anxieties keep you awake at night, wondering what terrible news tomorrow will bring? Fear is a very destructive emotion; it can make everything in your life fall apart.

That is why God not only frees you from your difficulties, but from the power of fear as well. How does he do so? First John 4:18 explains, "God's perfect love drives out fear" (NCV). He teaches you that anything that enters your life must first pass through his loving hand. If he allows a difficult situation to affect you, then he will most certainly use it for your good.

God, thank you for protecting me and teaching me courage through your wonderful love. Truly, with you, I have absolutely no reason to fear. Amen.

Therefore, do not be afraid. When you lie awake troubled by anxieties, turn your thoughts to his perfect love and allow him to calm your heart.

Those who look to him for help will be radiant with joy; no shadow of shame will darken their faces.

Psalm 34:5 NLT

HEIRLOOMS

God has made everything beautiful for its own time.

Ecclesiastes 3:11 NLT

Long ago, women's hands carefully crafted each block of a quilt. Each intricate shape made a perfect fit with the next, each section stitched together to create a breathtaking work of art. As a cherished family heirloom, the quilts displayed the skill, creativity, and love of those women who went before.

The expanse of the sky, the songs of the streams, the scent of a blossom testify to God's creative mind and living power. You are heir to a world full of magnificent reminders of who God is and what he can do. He encourages you to admire his creation, treasure it, and contemplate his continuing love for you.

Father in heaven: Thank you for the magnificence of the universe and the tender beauties of nature. I cherish the inheritance you have given me. Amen.

God looked over all that he had made, and it was excellent in every way.

Genesis 1:31 TLB

December 12

IN CONTROL

It is God who is at work in you, enabling you both to will and to work for his good pleasure.

Philippians 2:13 NRSV

All of us like to feel we exert some measure of control over the events of our lives, yet it takes only one completely unexpected turn to reveal the limits of our power and influence.

When you acknowledge God's supreme control, you equip yourself with the perspective you need to handle those times you must admit you have no control—when good plans fall through, when unforeseen trouble arises, when any move you make to change things proves futile. When you feel most powerless, you can smile, because God continues to take care of and handle those things that concern you. And he does so for your ultimate good.

Dear God: When events move beyond my control, help me rest in you, acknowledging my limitations and relying on you to see me through. Amen.

Letting the Spirit control your mind leads to life and peace.

Romans 8:6 NLT

December 13

STILLNESS IN HIM

A heart at peace gives life to the body.

Proverbs 14:30 NIV

Spiritual peace is not simply an absence of turmoil, but an exciting and multifaceted gift God desires to nurture in your heart.

The peace he offers supplies you with the strength it takes to confront life's tumultuous changes and formidable challenges. His peace includes his other spiritual gifts of faith and trust, wisdom, and confidence. When you accept it and let it reside within you, others cannot help but feel it, and they will be drawn to you.

Let God center his peace deep within you. When he does, you will experience the pleasure of stillness in him even during the most stressful of times.

The Lord will give His people peace.

Psalm 29:11 NLV

Dear God: Open my heart to your gift of peace that comes from putting my complete trust in you, knowing I have your peace always. Amen.

December 14

WORDS OF THE WISE

The godly offer good counsel; they teach right from wrong.
Psalm 37:30 NLT

When you are hurting, a friend's timely counsel can be a precious gift. Yet how can you discern if what she is telling you is godly and wise—or if it is foolish and destructive?

First, her words must line up with God's Word, never contradicting the principles of Scripture. Second, her instruction should direct you to the Lord and encourage you to honor him completely. Third, whether she is offering you comfort or correction, she should not be fishing for a certain response. Rather, she must be honest, compassionate, and tactful so you can grow in your faith.

Sometimes it will be obvious that a friend's advice is straight from God, but when it is not, turn her words over to him in prayer. He will certainly show you whether it is worthwhile counsel or not.

God, please help me discern whether the advice I receive and give is godly and wise. I want to honor you, Lord, especially in the counsel I give to others. Amen.

Look at those who are honest and good, for a wonderful future awaits those who love peace.

Psalm 37:37 NLT

December 15

YOUR CREATIVE LIGHT

God created human beings in his image. In the image of God he created them.

Genesis 1:27 NCV

A potter uses her hands to sculpt a bowl of extraordinary beauty. A dancer enthralls the audience with expressive movements. A poet touches hearts with evocative phrases. All these are expressions of creativity. But if you really want to see a dazzling display of creativity, consider this:

In you, God has fashioned a home for his Spirit, and through the presence of his Spirit, your voice, hands, and feet express your unique ways of worshiping him. Through thoughtful words and compassionate actions, you mold relationships. Through the careful attention you bring to even the smallest of tasks, you evoke an aura of loveliness and peace. In God, your creativity shines.

Creator-God: Keep my heart and mind full of thoughts, ideas, and dreams that flow into creative expressions of love. Amen.

I worship in adoration—what a creation!

Psalm 139:14 THE MESSAGE

REAL, ABUNDANT LIFE

With you is the fountain of life; in your light do we see light.

Psalm 36:9 ESV

What does the perfect life look like to you? Perhaps you picture a life of wealth and luxury. Or maybe you desire to be surrounded by loved ones, people who care deeply about you. Although there is nothing wrong with these dreams, when you finally reach them, you will most likely find that there is still something missing.

John 17:3 explains, "Eternal life is to know you, the only true God, and to know Jesus Christ" (CEV). That is because when you seek God, you will find a truly worthwhile life, not only full of purpose but also full of love, hope, and meaning.

God, I need you in my life. Your presence makes all things more wonderfully satisfying—including family, friendships, and all this life has to offer. Amen.

Friend, do you feel as if something is missing from your life? Pursue God. Love him. Devote yourself to him. He will satisfy your heart's deepest desires and never disappoint you.

Your love, O Lord, reaches to the heavens, your faithfulness to the skies. . . . How priceless is your unfailing love! Both high and low among men find refuge in the shadow of your wings.

Psalm 36:5, 7 NIV

December 17

EVERYDAY WONDERS

Christ made everything in the heavens and on the earth.

Colossians 1:16 NLV

A small child enthralled by the feel of grass and the sight of wildflowers grew up to become an accomplished nature artist.

Today, take a few moments to notice the simple wonders of nature. Watch clouds floating, listen to leaves rustling in the wind, delight in the rose's fragrance and fresh-cut grass. Pick up a pebble, twig, or shell to keep where you'll see it every day, and let yourself become enthralled and enchanted by the gift of God's creation. You don't need to be an accomplished artist to see the beauty in nature. You just need to see God's work in all the world around you.

Take a good look at God's wonders—they'll take your breath away.

Psalm 66:5 THE MESSAGE

Creator-God: Thank you for the beauty and magnificence of creation. Open the eyes of my spirit to see and appreciate the natural wonders around me every day. Amen.

December 18

A BEAUTIFUL WORK OF ART

I will praise You, because I have been remarkably and wonderfully made. Your works are wonderful.

Psalm 139:14 HCSB

No matter what you think of yourself or what anyone else has ever said, the fact is that you are a masterpiece of God. Perhaps you reject this truth because of many painful experiences. Or maybe you think that if you had a certain beauty treatment, lost some weight, or had better clothes, you would be okay.

God loves you just the way you are. When he put you together, he was delighted with the person he created.

Are you perfect? No. But you are loved by the One who is. So instead of thinking of the things that make you unique as negatives, look at them for what they really are—details that make you God's special work of art.

God, sometimes it is difficult to think of myself in a positive way. Thank you for seeing me as beautiful. Please teach me to see myself as you do—a masterpiece. Amen.

You created my inmost being. . . . Your eyes saw my unformed body. All the days ordained for me were written in your book before one of them came to be.

Psalm 139:13, 16 NIV

DENYING THE DRAMA QUEEN WITHIN

Do you want to live and enjoy a long life? Then don't say cruel things and don't tell lies. Do good instead of evil and try to live at peace.

Psalm 34:12–14 CEV

"Go ahead, get it out of your system," your friends urge during some trial. So you do. You allow the emotions to pour forth. You spout things you do not really mean, and you blow your troubles out of proportion. You feel better for a moment.

> *God, I do not need drama in my life—I need your peace. Please forgive me for spouting off. Help me to deal with my emotions in a way that honors you. Amen.*

Then the feelings come back stronger than ever, and they are even more painful and harder to shake off. What happened?

The problem is not that you have expressed your emotions; it is that you have allowed them to run amok. Now you are trapped by the drama you have created.

That is why whenever something difficult comes into your life, you must seek God's understanding about it. Express yourself to him and allow his wisdom to guide you. The less dramatic route will lead you to peace.

The Lord is close to the brokenhearted, and he saves those whose spirits have been crushed. People who do what is right may have many problems, but the Lord will solve them all.

Psalm 34:18–19 NCV

WHOLE YOU

May God himself, the God who makes everything holy and whole, make you holy and whole, put you together—spirit, soul, and body.

1 Thessalonians 5:23 THE MESSAGE

*G*od has been called the Great Physician for good reason—wherever he finds a broken spirit, he works to heal and make things whole again.

Your innermost private wounds are known by God, and you cannot hide them from his restorative touch. Instead, he draws you close to him, caressing you with the balm of his comfort, bathing you in the cleansing waters of forgiveness, and embracing you in complete wholeness of spirit and soul.

Whenever your heart weeps because of wounds from the past or sorrows suffered today, step close to God, the Great Physician of body and soul. He will heal you.

I am the Lord who heals you.

Exodus 15:26 NKJV

Great Physician: There are broken places in my life, and I need your creative and re-creative touch for the wholeness only you have the power to bring about in my life. Amen.

GOD'S GOOD WILL

The world and its desires pass away, but the man who does the will of God lives forever.

1 John 2:17 NIV

It's God's will" is a phrase often spoken with a sigh over the sadness of loss. The closer you come to understanding God's will, however, the more likely you are to exclaim joyfully, "It's God's will!" as you consider the good things he makes happen in your life.

God, in his boundless love for you, reveals his will to you so you can make your choices and decisions in accordance with it. He urges you to learn more about his good purposes for you by studying the Bible. He wants you to follow his will, and know that it is the path to true happiness.

Teach me to do your will, for you are my God. May your gracious Spirit lead me forward on a firm footing.

Psalm 143:10 NLT

Heavenly Father: Thank you for making your will known to me. Grant me wisdom that I may take pleasure in following the good plans you have for my life. Amen.

December 22

JOY OF SALVATION

[God] declared us righteous and gave us confidence that we will inherit eternal life.

Titus 3:7 NLT

*Y*ou possess the God-given ability to enjoy life, because God has rescued you from wondering what will happen to you at the end of life. He invites you to place your trust in his promise of salvation and life everlasting.

Your deliverance from the grip of spiritual death sets you free from fear and misgivings about the future, and helps you to accept the passing of your Christian loved ones because of the sure knowledge you will rejoice with them again in heaven. Just imagine the pleasure of seeing again their eyes and their smiles, and hearing the sound of their voices!

The joy of salvation is joy for today.

[God] alone is my rock and my salvation; he is my fortress, I will never be shaken.

Psalm 62:2 NIV

Heavenly Father: Grant me the certainty of your complete deliverance from spiritual death so I may spend my days in joyful expectation of the life to come in you. Amen.

COMPLIMENTS DUE

God takes particular pleasure in acts of worship—a different kind of "sacrifice"—that takes place in kitchen and workplace and on the streets.

Hebrews 13:16 THE MESSAGE

*S*tudies have shown how receiving deserved compliments increases self-confidence and enhances self-esteem. Studies rarely mention, however, the benefits accrued by the person offering praise.

God, in his magnificence and perfection, does not need to be complimented, but he wants us to receive the benefits that come our way when we show appreciation for who he is and what he does.

When you acknowledge his greatness, you heighten your awareness of your humanity and your need for his help and strength. You also strengthen your faith by acknowledging that God is good and great and powerful enough to come to your aid. Give praise and open your heart to be blessed.

Dear God: Thank you for revealing yourself to me, and thank you for inviting me to join the heavens in worshiping you. Amen.

I will be glad and exult in you; I will sing praise to your name, O Most High.

Psalm 9:2 NRSV

EXCHANGING TRIALS FOR GLORY

My whole being will exclaim, "Who is like you, O Lord?"

Psalm 35:10 NIV

*I*f you are strong or gifted enough to accomplish a task, what room is there for God to work? If you can personally guarantee a successful conclusion to the assignment you face, what need is there for faith?

That is why God will challenge you beyond what you can handle. It is only when you cannot manage your circumstances that you acknowledge God's hand. Any success you achieve is from God. Of course, no one likes to relinquish control, but that is what it takes to see his astounding work in your life.

God, I want to know you, but I am afraid of losing control. Teach me to respond to situations in a way that honors you and helps me grow in your love. Amen.

Are you committed to following him no matter what it takes? Are you willing to encounter trials in exchange for experiencing his glory? When you are, you will truly get to know him, and that is definitely worth it.

Those who want the best for me, let them have the last word—a glad shout!—and say, over and over and over, "God is great—everything works together for good for his servant."

Psalm 35:27 THE MESSAGE

EXPERIENCE HIS SPIRIT

*We have not received the spirit of the world but the Spirit who is from
God, that we may understand what God has freely given us.*

1 Corinthians 2:12 NIV

Imagine strolling on a woodland path and discovering a
small bench nestled among the trees. As you sit for a few
moments, the breathtaking peace of the forest comes over you and
infuses your soul with its sweetness. You're humbled at once by the
honor of being who you are in this time and place.

As you walk in relationship with God, there will be moments
when you're stirred by a startling awareness of the Holy Spirit
living, breathing, and working in you. The humbling experience
leaves you without words to express your
new understanding, but with a deeper
conviction that God has, indeed, chosen
you to be his dwelling place.

*Dear God: Grant me
faithfulness on my
walk with your Spirit,
and open me to the
humbling awareness
of you in my heart and
in my life. Amen.*

Do you not know that your body is a temple of the Holy Spirit who is in you, whom
you have from God?

1 Corinthians 6:19 NASB

LIFE OF PLENTY

God will generously provide all you need. Then you will always have everything you need and plenty left over to share with others.

2 Corinthians 9:8 NLT

The Bible tells of a destitute widow and her son who encountered the prophet Elijah as she was preparing a meal with the last of her oil and flour. A severe famine left little hope for more. Nevertheless, Elijah asked her the unthinkable—use what you have left to bake me a loaf of bread. Out of respect for God she did as he asked and quickly found her flour and oil containers were miraculously refilled each time she ran out.

Through all the circumstances and opportunities of your life, God sees to your needs, and he invites you to take pleasure in his provisions by sharing generously with others.

Dear God: Allow me many opportunities to give of my time, effort, and provisions so I may truly enjoy and appreciate all you have given to me. Amen.

"My people will be filled with My goodness," says the Lord.

Jeremiah 31:14 NLV

MAKING DISCIPLES

No discipline is enjoyable while it is happening—it is painful! But afterward there will be a peaceful harvest of right living for those who are trained in this way.

Hebrews 12:11 NLT

The mother who disciplines her children in a loving and consistent manner earns their heartfelt respect and gratitude. They learn she cares about them enough to guide and instruct them as they grow.

God cares so much about you that he makes it known when you are veering away from his will for your life. He corrects you for the purpose of bringing you back and strengthening you, teaching and training you. When you receive God's instruction, gladly accept it and learn from it, because his voice of authority is a sure indication that he sees you as one of his own precious children.

My child, don't make light of the Lord's discipline, and don't give up when he corrects you. For the Lord disciplines those he loves.

Hebrews 12:5–6 NLT

Heavenly Father: Thank you for the times you have corrected me and brought me back to you. I want to learn to grow and walk in discipleship. Amen.

EXTRAORDINARY DAYS

Happy are those who hear the joyful call to worship, for they will walk in the light of your presence, Lord.

Psalm 89:15 NLT

When you're with someone you love, even ordinary activities take on the glow of happiness. Spend a few moments now to meditate on God's compassionate presence in your life and his unfailing love for you.

In the Bible, God declares himself immersed in the lives of his loved ones so each person may know the pleasure of his company. God's presence in your life means you carry his guiding light with you wherever you go and you can enjoy his divine companionship, even during the most mundane tasks on the most ordinary days.

Of course, in his extraordinary presence, there's no such thing as an ordinary day!

You have upheld me because of my integrity, and set me in your presence forever.

Psalm 41:12 NRSV

Heavenly Father: Thank you for the gift of your presence in my life, because with you all my days are infused with purpose and pleasure. I delight in your companionship. Amen.

TRUE VINE

Whoever pursues righteousness and kindness will find life and honor.

Proverbs 21:21 NRSV

To her consternation, a gardener discovered a climbing weed had entangled itself in a favored vine. The only way she could tell the weed from the vine was by examining the leaves.

In the world, genuine believers live and work right alongside name-only Christians, and from a distance, it may be difficult to tell the difference. Up close, however, all you need to do is examine words and actions—genuine Christianity exhibits itself in a God-pleasing lifestyle and an obvious desire to grow in Christlikeness.

Take a few moments to consider how the "leaves" of your life reveal that you belong to Jesus, who has said, "I am the vine."

> *Dear God: Cultivate in me a sincere desire to walk in uprightness of heart so that my words and actions will show I belong to you. Amen.*

The ways of right-living people glow with light; the longer they live, the brighter they shine.

Proverbs 4:18 THE MESSAGE

THE DELIGHT
OF CREATING

The Lord made the heavens and everything in them by his word.

Psalm 33:6 CEV

God takes joy in creating. He loves inventing worlds of delight for you.

First, he plants a desire in you—a seed that he lovingly nurtures. Undoubtedly, some special hope comes to mind. You know that it originated with him because it is impossible to achieve without him. You know that when it is accomplished, he will receive all the glory and praise.

Then, he creates conditions for that hope to mature and blossom. He delights in growing it into something that is above and beyond what you could imagine. And he loves to see your joyous face when you finally grasp the delightful things he created just for you.

God, you are my joy. Just as you created the world by your word, I know you are powerfully inventing good things for me. Amen.

Delight yourself also in the Lord, and He will give you the desires and secret petitions of your heart.

Psalm 37:4 AMP

PATIENCE, FRIEND

Entrust your ways to the Lord. Trust him, and he will act on your behalf. . . . Surrender yourself to the Lord, and wait patiently for him.

Psalm 37:5, 7 GOD'S WORD

It can be very frustrating. You get ready to work, but the inspiration is just not there. You need to get things done to stay on track, but something prevents you from moving forward.

Friend, God is waiting for you to get quiet before him, to cast aside your worries and seek the peace of his presence. After all, what you are doing is for him; he is not going to fail you. However, learning to trust him is more important than whatever you must get done.

> *Lord, waiting is a challenge! Help me to be patient. Help me to know you better and trust you more so that I may serve you wholeheartedly and please you. Amen.*

Therefore, take a deep breath and calm your heart. Express your absolute confidence that he will do as he has promised. He will help you in your work and provide the desires of your heart. Then wait patiently for him to inspire you, because he will certainly do wonderful things on your behalf.

Trust in the Lord, and do good; dwell in the land, and feed on His faithfulness. Delight yourself also in the Lord, and He shall give you the desires of your heart.

Psalm 37:3–4 NKJV